Why

They
Just
Don't Understand

and

How You
Can Help.

www.notsostupidparents.com

Stupid Parents

Why They Just Don't Understand
and How You Can Help

Hayley DiMarco

Revell
Grand Rapids, Michigan

Hungry Planet

Published by Fleming H. Revell
a division of Baker Publishing Group
P.O. Box 6287, Grand Rapids, MI 49516-6287
www.revellbooks.com

Printed in the United States of America

Library of Congress Cataloging-in-Publication Data
DiMarco, Hayley.
    Stupid parents : why they just don't understand and how you can help / Hayley DiMarco
        p.   cm.
    ISBN 10: 0-8007-3151-4 (pbk.)
    ISBN 978-0-8007-3151-9 (pbk.)
    1. Christian teenagers—Religious life. 2. Parent and teenager—Religious aspects—Christianity. I. Title.
    BV4531.3.D56 2006
    248.8'3—dc22   2006011107

Scripture is taken from the *Holy Bible*, New Living Translation, copyright © 1996. Used by permission of Tyndale House Publishers, Inc., Wheaton, IL 60189. All rights reserved.

Published in association with Yates & Yates, LLP, Literary Agents, Orange, California.

Contents

Part 3 **The Big Talk** *Ever have something really important to tell your parents but don't know how? Find out ways to say what you want to say without turning it into a major knockdown drag-out.*

Part 4 **Rebuilding Broken Trust** *What happens if you've blown it and now they don't trust you? Is there a way back to how things were? Here's the quickest way back to Normalsville.*

Part 5 **Really Stupid Parents** *Sometimes parents are doing things they shouldn't, not to you but around you—and they cause you trauma. Are your parents messing up so bad they're making you wish you weren't related?*

Part 6 **Living with a Single Parent** *Things are totally different when it comes to living with only one parent. It might be a huge change to you or the same ole same ole. Either way there are some big pitfalls you both need to try to avoid.*

The End—*or as Some Call It, the Conclusion.*

Honor your father and mother.
Then you will live a long, full life.

—the 5th
Commandment
(Exodus 20:12)

Introduction

Meet My Stupid Parents

For being so old, they sure can be clueless. Why do parents seem so out of touch sometimes? It's like they're just plain stupid. If you've ever yelled at your parents, slammed the door, walked out on them, or said, "My parents are so stupid!" then you've come to the right place. *Stupid Parents* **is going to make your life better.** For centuries kids have decided that their parents just don't get life anymore. It's like they lose brain cells as they get older and can't for the life of them remember what it was like to be a teenager. But is that really the case, or is there something much more elusive at work?

What if you could learn how to get your parents to get you? What if you could get them to lighten up and understand more

The Other S Word

stupid: a bad word used to describe someone you don't currently like, who is frustrating you, or who just doesn't understand

Parents hate this word, especially when it describes them, so try to avoid it at all costs. And if they don't like the title of this book, explain that you don't think they're stupid; you just wish they understood you better, and this book is supposed to help.

about who you are and who you want to be? It can be done, you know; it really can. Parents and teenagers can get along and get things done. It just takes a little tweaking.

In these pages you aren't going to read that your parents are always right. You aren't going to read that they know everything and you are just too young to get it. But you are going to read some things that should drastically change the way you talk to them and interact with them. See, here's the thing: **If you keep doing what you're doing, you'll keep getting what you're getting.** And my question to you is, "Is that enough?" If you love the status quo, then close this book. But if you want to change the way your life is at home, then keep reading.

Meet My Mom

My mom can drive me crazy. I mean, how hard is it to download an attachment off of email? Believe me, very hard, if you're my mother. Don't get me wrong; my mom is great. She's so kind and caring. She always took such good care of me. She loves me. She fed and clothed me and acted as both mom and dad to me. She's a jewel. But sometimes she can drive me nuts. And I have to confess that I haven't always been the nicest person in return. I lose my patience with her. I've yelled. I've huffed and I've puffed. Everything short of blowing the house down. And I know she hates it. It has put a strain on our relationship. So believe me, I understand when you think your parents just don't get it. Today I would never call my mom stupid, even if she can't figure out how to reboot or defrag her computer, but when I was in high school I wanted to. Truth is, she is very bright; she's just not part of my generation, so a lot of new things stump her. I mean, she didn't grow up with computers in the classroom. More like pencils and slide rules. Ugh! It's no wonder she doesn't get stuff, but boy, can I get frustrated by her inability to get it.

It seems like the parent-child relationship can be the most exasperating of all relationships, probably because we're so close to each other and in each other's faces for so many hours a day. If you're like me and you want some peace at home, then have hope. It can be done—it just might take a little work and a little understanding. So keep on keeping on, and we'll see if we can't get the stupid out of the parent.

The Perfect Parents

Fact or Fiction?

PART 1

The perfect parents: fact or fiction? Well, I'm guessing that if you're reading this book, you probably think they're fiction. I mean, sure, you might have heard the random kid say, "I have the *best* parents!" but you just rolled your eyes in disbelief or disgust. Or maybe you dream of being able to say that. **Parents can be sheer trauma.** They can make your life miserable, but they can also make your life amazing. Sometimes it can vary from day to day or mood to mood. Truth is, no one is perfect, and when you live that close to someone, you are bound to find some friction. Kids the world over are continually heard saying, "My parents are so stupid! They just don't understand." So trust me, **you're not alone.**

Why So Clueless?

Truth be told, **the perfect parents don't exist.** That's because no perfect people exist. And before you forget, your parents are just human. They aren't the superhumans you thought they were when you were a little kid. And that might be why the friction has started for you—because **you're growing up and you're seeing their flaws.** You're smart enough to know now that they aren't invincible, they aren't all-knowing, and they aren't perfect. The older you get, the more you see their flaws and the more you start to think they just don't get it. Heck with calling them "the smartest people on earth," like you used to when you were 5. Now they just seem totally clueless.

And to some extent that's true. They *are* clueless. They can't figure out how to create their own website. They don't know the

breakout artist of the year. They haven't a clue about text messaging or what jeans are all the rage this year. They are out of touch, and for good reason. **When they were in school things were different.** Technology is racing so fast they can't always keep up with it. And fashion—who has time for fashion when they have to keep the lights on and dinner on the table? So when you start to talk, sometimes they glaze over in confusion, clueless as to what you are talking about. And truth be told, that's the worst for them. It's awful not to be able to understand stuff. They start to feel old, and no one wants that. Heck, **they** *feel* **like they are still in their 20s**, but every time you outknow them in something, they start to feel their age, and that's uncomfortable.

Another reason they can't be perfect is because **they are making a lot of life up on the fly.** I mean, when you have kids they don't give you any parent manual that takes care of everything. Most parents are trying their best with the skills they have to do what they can for you. They learned from their parents, who learned from their parents, and so on. And a lot of times what they learned is "I don't want to do it like that." So they are attempting to find ways to make your life better than theirs was. Believe me when I say your parents might not be perfect, but they do want what's best for you.

Psycho Parents

The world does have the occasional crazy parent who really isn't safe. This is the abuser, the parent who hurts you physically. And I'm not talking spanking here; I'm talking about throwing-you-against-the-wall rage. If your parent isn't rational, you need to seek help. This book might have some pointers for you that can help you learn to avoid their wrath, but don't overlook the need for intervention. No one has a right to cause you physical harm.

EveryBoDy Gets olD

We can't overlook the fact that your parents are just plain getting old, and getting old takes its toll. I mean, talk about tired! Your body just gets more and more achy and tired the older you get. And they seem to still have so much to do that sometimes they can feel just plain overwhelmed. So if they seem extra grumpy, it might be because they are just exhausted. I hate to say it, although probably not as much as you'll hate to hear it, but that's why when you help your parents out by doing things around the house, you greatly reduce their fatigue and therefore their likelihood to be angry or nagging. Not sure how to do that when all you want is just to live your life? Stay tuned, plenty of ideas are coming up in the pages to follow.

Another cause of conflict in your family life, besides your parents' inability to be on the cutting edge of life, is the fact that you are growing up, and growing up means independence. It means that you start to test how well you can handle yourself on your own. You test the waters to see if what your parents taught you is true for you. You start to break out on your own, make your own decisions, and form your own thoughts. And this can be a rough transition for parents who still think of you as their baby. Besides making them feel old, to have almost an adult living where they used to have a child also makes them scared to think of you breaking out on your own. That's why they can seem overprotective. A lot of times they are scared they've done something wrong and haven't taught you all you need, and that might be why they overreact when you do something wrong. They often blame themselves.

Whatever the situation, **it's just plain hard for parents to see their babies growing up.** And that can cause friction. So give them a break and try to understand that all they are feeling is a deep love and concern for you and worry about their ability or inability to care for you as you grow into an independent adult.

The Complete Family Makeover

So if the perfect parents don't exist, **is it even possible to have a complete family makeover that can change the war at home between you and your parentals?** The answer: yes. You can have a better family life, and that transformation might just rest in your hands.

I know, and I hope you do as well, that you can't *change* your parents. Truth be told, you can't change anyone but yourself. Have you ever tried to control someone or get them to do what they didn't want to do? If so, then you can "amen" my line of thinking. Changing others is a colossal waste of time because it can't be done unless they are willing participants. Anyone who spends their precious energy trying to change someone else is in for serious heartache. So that leaves us with ourselves. The true power to change the fam rests inside of you, since you're a part of it. It's really kind of a cool thing since you have so much power over yourself. With a few minor tweaks to the way you interact with your parentals, you could potentially end arguing and nagging forever.

Could it be true? Is it possible to have the perfect parental relationship just by looking inward? Yeppers. You have more power than you might realize in this relationship. In the pages that follow, I'm going to give you pointers to help you get what you want out of your relationship with your parents. I'm going to teach you about authority and how to manage yourself under it in order to make your life better. When it comes to dealing with someone who has control over you, like parents, teachers, or bosses, it helps to learn where your strength lies and about a little something called the art of the deal. By the time you get done with this book, you should be ready to handle all the ups and downs of the parental relationship much more happily than you are right now.

The Art of the Deal

PART 2

Who's the Boss?

Anyone who has authority over you always has the final say. They hold the position of power. That's the way it is for your parents and their bosses, for the fry cook at the Super Slurp, and for you with your parents. **Learning now how to deal with people who control major aspects of your life will pay off throughout your life.** It can affect how much money you make, what kind of jobs you get and keep, and how comfortable you are at home.

Before we get started on the good stuff, let's look at **two stupid ways people react to the authorities in their life:**

1. Quitting

2. Overpowering

Quitters Never Win

When it comes to a job, you can always quit if you don't like your boss. I used to know a girl who would quit every time her boss did or said something she didn't like. And each time she would have to hit the pavement and find another job, starting all over at the bottom of the pay scale. Because of her constant discontent with people in authority over her, she never stayed anywhere long enough to move up. She never made more money or got a better position. She always stayed at the bottom of the ladder and just jumped from one ladder to another.

Now, it was her choice to jump ship when the orders from the captain got to be too much for her to handle, and that's the beauty of a job. You can move to another one any time you like. But when it comes to your parents, you don't have that luxury. You can't tell them you quit and move to the house next door every time they tick you off. You're stuck with the ones you've got. Face it, the parents you've got are the parents you'll always have. Sure, if your parents are split, you can change locations once, but most people I know who have done this tell me they run into the same problems with authority with parent #2. So unless you have a huge trust fund independent of your parents' control, **it's probably best to figure them out rather than bailing out on them** and doing it all on your own or spending all your free time arguing with them over stupid stuff.

Face it, the parents you've got are the parents you'll always have.

OverPowering Your Parents?

Another stupid way some people try to handle someone in authority over them is by trying to overpower them, to take over the relationship, to wrangle the power away from them. Let's just make it crystal clear right now: Any attempt to overcome the power of those in authority over you—parents, teachers, bosses, police, etc.—is a giant waste of your time. Think of it like this. When you go to McDonald's in the middle of the afternoon and want the Big Breakfast, you can't overcome the fact that they won't give it to you. You don't have the power to change the hours they serve breakfast. And believe me, any attempt to do so is futile. They just look at you with a blank look and say, "Sorry, no hotcakes for you!" It can't be done. The same goes for your job. You can't set corporate policy or the hours you work. And many an idiot has tried to overcome the power of the police only to end up facedown on the ground looking at his reflection in those shiny black boots. Face it, **if you try to overpower the authority in your life, you lose.**

The same goes for parents. Like it or not, they control things, and any attempt to take that power from them can only make things worse. That's just the way it is, and the sooner you figure that out, the better. You don't pay the bills, they do—hence the power thing. So understanding your position is crucial. Only when you know your position can you start to make the relationship better. So the first thing I want you to do is to stop thinking that in order to be happy, you have to overcome the power and control of your parents. Giant waste-o of time-o, chico!

Let's Make a Deal!

Instead of wasting your time and energy trying to change your parents, let's see if we can't get our arms around what I call *the art of the deal*. The object of deal-making is to change the situation so everyone feels like they are getting what they want, or at least something close to it. I mean, you can't keep winning all the time and expect the other person to want to keep playing with you. Losing isn't fun, and doing it over and over again is the worst. But you probably don't feel much like the winner right now. In fact, you're probably sick and tired of always losing the arguments and always being told what to do, and you want a shift in the results.

The truth is that your parents probably feel the same way. If there is friction in your relationship, then believe me, they don't feel like they're winning either, even if they ultimately *do* get you to do what they want. The struggle to get there is not something they look forward to every day either. So for starters, understand that **they have something to gain from ending the friction too.** If they can come home at the end of a long day and not have to yell at you or argue with you, then they will feel like they've won. What they want is for you to do the right thing (which is usually whatever it is *they* want) with as little drama as possible. They're tired. They're overworked. And the last thing they want is another argument. So don't forget that. It's part of what can give you a little power of your own. Understanding what you have or can offer another person is called leverage, and you can use it with your parents just like in a business deal. But finding out what they really want is crucial, because if you don't give them what they want, or at least try to work toward it, the battles will continue to rage.

The second thing you have to grasp is that *your* actions greatly affect what happens to you. It's the cause and effect thing. You might feel powerless sometimes, like life just comes at you and you have nothing to do with what happens, but that isn't always the case. So before we start into the heart of the art of the deal, let's take a quick look at your actions and their negative or positive results and see if we can find a pattern. Again, if what you're doing hasn't been working, then the smart thing to do is to change what you're doing. Here's what I want you to do. Write down some of the ways you react to your parents and then the results of those ways you react. Like this:

YOUR REACTION	THEIR RESPONSE
Slam the door when she starts to yell at me	She yells louder
Look bored when she's talking	She gets mad at me
Ignore him	He gets mad

See the cause and effect thing? You might think that no matter what, they are going to get mad at you, and that's just the way it is. But that's not the case. They are responding to you. It's human nature. Everyone reacts and responds to the way people talk to and treat them, even parents. So check it out: What if you changed your reaction? Do you think by chance you might get a different response from them? Maybe, maybe not. But anything is worth a try when things aren't going your way, huh? So let's keep on chipping away at this stuff to see if we can't figure out the solution to your dilemma.

When it comes to the art of the deal, it's important to realize what kind of commodity you are dealing with—that is, what you have that *they* want. In order to do that, let's look at a few scenarios and see if we can't start to understand more about why parents do what they do and how you can help to get a better result out of the relationship.

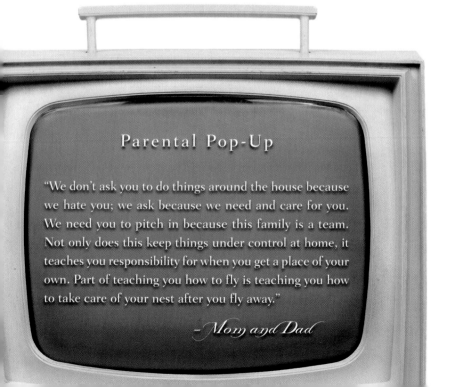

Parental Pop-Up

"We don't ask you to do things around the house because we hate you; we ask because we need and care for you. We need you to pitch in because this family is a team. Not only does this keep things under control at home, it teaches you responsibility for when you get a place of your own. Part of teaching you how to fly is teaching you how to take care of your nest after you fly away."

– Mom and Dad

Stop the Nagging

Being nagged is so lame. **I mean, how old are you? Seven?** It's not like you didn't hear them the first time or you don't know what they want. Why do they have to ask you over and over again? When parents nag, you feel talked down to and run ragged. You have a busy schedule too, and fitting what *they* want into it isn't always easy. Your life doesn't seem like your own because they are continually micromanaging you, as if you can't do it on your own. "Pick up your room." "Get to your homework." "Unload the dishwasher." "Blah, blah, blah!" The continual barrage of orders feels more like boot camp than the comfort of home, your crash pad. They don't understand the pressure you are under because they didn't have the same kind of pressure when they were your age. They forget how tired you can get and how much you just want to rest. They don't understand how important your friendships are and how much work it takes just to care for them. And mostly they just want things done—no, they *need* things done.

Your parents have an idea of how life at home should be, and they want you to conform to it. So when you don't do it the way they want and on their time schedule, they nag, and you break. "I know, I know," you mumble as you leave the room. "I *will*! Just lay off!" you shout as you slam your door. And the battle rages on.

So what's the art of the deal have to say about this situation? What are the elements of this dilemma that can be played with and tweaked in order to get both you and your parents what you want so the shouting can cease?

1. Nagging happens because they feel like they have to ask you over and over again to do something. They have to ask you over and over again because you didn't do anything the *first* time they asked you.

Mr. Obvious says: "So do it the first time they ask you!"

Sure, that makes the most sense. Do it the first time. If you can make a point of doing what they ask right when they ask you, then you can avoid tons of nagging. I mean, what can they nag you about if you did what they asked? Trouble is, you don't always feel like you have time to do it right when they ask. You have a life, other things that have to get done, so you can't always do it *right that second*. And parents don't always understand that. So

Parental Pop-Up

"I used to think I was busy until I not only had my own stuff to do like work and shopping but added the responsibility of kids and a husband. At the end of the day I am exhausted, and I really feel like I need my daughter's help with stuff around the house or I'm going to literally collapse. It's especially hard on days when my boss has yelled at me. I just want to come home and crawl under the covers, but I can't do that. I have responsibilities now."

—Mom

the next day they ask again, thinking you must have forgotten or you would have done it. And if you don't do it this time, they really blow their top because they've asked you twice and you still didn't do anything. In their minds they are thinking, *How hard is it to do what I've asked?* Their reasoning goes something like this: "When I'm at work and I get asked to do something by my boss, I'd darn well better do it or I'll lose my job." It's just the way their minds work—when asked by someone in authority over you to do something, you do it. They might work overtime, go in early, or complain about their workload continually because *they*, just like you, are being told what to do by someone who has power over them. Only for them, if they don't do it, it could mean getting fired, whereas for you, there's no chance of that. But that's part of their frustration. If you can't learn *now* how to do things when you're asked, then how will you ever hold down a job where you're being asked to do stuff all day long? How will you support yourself when you're ready to go out on your own? See, **their nagging isn't all about bossing you around.** It's one part needing your help to get things done and one part wanting to teach you some skills so you can get and keep that killer job that you're going to want in order to get out on your own.

You might be playing your itty-bitty violin between your fingers right now and saying, "Would you like more cheese with your whine?" But whether you care about their trials and worries or not, you need to trust me on this: **Knowing where they are coming from and what they are feeling will help you in the art of the deal.** Remember, it's all about figuring out what they want or need in order to better get what you want or need. It's like the market economy you learned about in social studies. If you have what someone else wants or can supply some kind of service that they need, then you can sell them that good or ser-

7 Things You Should Never Do When Being Nagged

Never roll your eyes.

Never say, "Stop nagging!"

Never turn your back to them.

Never say, "I know, I know!"

Never try to outshout them.

Never use the word *stupid*.

Never cover your ears and sing "I'm not listening!"

vice in order to get what you want or need in return. In the family environment the exchange of goods and services is not just for money but for something sometimes far more valuable—peace and quiet. You want it, and they'll give it to you if you give them what they want. Win-win! So how do you give them what they want and still keep your sanity in your busy, busy world?

Mr. Obvious says: "Please, don't ever let them see you playing your itty-bitty violin between your fingers in front of them. Not the best way to stay on their good side."

2. Ignoring them just makes it worse. They sound like a broken record. You've heard it before, so you shut them off. Just ignore them. It seems to make more sense. I mean, why listen to the nagging when all it does is frustrate you? But I've got news for ya—when you ignore them, you only make it worse. It's like this: If I'm in a closed-in stairwell at school and the doors are all locked, I'm going to start knocking to see if anyone can let me out. And if I can hear them talking on the other side of the door so I know they are there but they are just ignoring me, I'm going to start yelling at them and pounding on the door. And if they still don't open it for me, I'm going to start yelling and pounding even louder. The more they ignore me, the louder I get, because I want to get out of there. Catch the visual? When you think you are being ignored or someone can't hear you, you talk or yell even louder.

Same goes for the nagging. When you ignore their requests, especially if they've been repeated, then they feel like they need to keep on you because you aren't listening. It's a frustrating experience not to be listened to. I'm sure you know what I'm talking about. For me, it's probably the worst feeling in the world. You know when you're trying to tell somebody something or prove a point and they just keep saying "Yeah, yeah, whatever" and try to talk over you or act like they won't listen to you? That drives me nuts! I used to start screaming and getting in their face. It makes me feel so helpless; I just want to grab them by the shoulders and shake them to make them listen. Sound familiar? It's awful not to be listened to. So don't ignore your parents when they ask you stuff. You only make things harder on yourself. Instead, here's what I want you to do:

3. Shut up. Yep, I know it's hard, but shut up. Listen to them. Hear what they want from you without saying, "But Mom . . . !" When you shut up, you make things a lot easier on yourself.

4. Listen to them. Okay, now that your mouth is shut, hear them out. Let them tell you what they want and why. It makes them feel better. And when they feel better, you'll feel better. It's part of the market economy. Treat your customers with respect, and they will continue to come back for more. If you want to do repeat business with your parents, then treat them well, and you'll be amazed how much more freedom you will get.

5. Look 'em in the eyes. Adults *love* this. When you look an adult in the eyes, they feel listened to. But more importantly, it makes you look more like an adult. Little kids let their eyes wander, and it makes them look immature, unable to handle responsibility and important stuff. You want them to respect you and start to treat you like an adult? Then above all else, look 'em in the eyes. All adults. Your parents, your teachers, the bank teller, the police officer. Everyone. Always look them in the eyes, and you'll go up a notch on the respect-o-meter.

6. Apologize. When you get nagged, apologize. Tell them you are sorry you didn't do it earlier. Making excuses doesn't help the situation. So when you *briefly* explain *why* you didn't do what they asked, don't whine and try to make them feel sorry for you. Remember, this is supposed to sound like an apology. I know you desperately want to prove to them that you had more important things to do, but be careful, because trying to fight for your rights only ticks them off more, and then you lose. So keep it short and just apologize for not doing it sooner "because (fill in the blank)." No whining! You only want them to hear that you had a conflict but that you are sorry. This can stave off a potential battle before it starts.

7. Feel for them. The next step is to make them feel better by showing them you understand their frustration—that way they don't have to explain it to *you*. This avoids a lecture. When you try to understand where they are coming from and tell them you do, they no longer have anything to lecture you about. So tell them you understand how frustrating it must be to them and how you understand that they really wanted this or that thing done. If you can sympathize with people, you can get a lot further in life. It causes them to let down their guard. Especially your parents—they won't know what to think of your newfound sensitivity. It's definitely a great bargaining chip in the art of the deal. But be genuine; they don't need to know that you're bargaining. Try to

Top 10 Reasons Parents Nag

Chores

Homework

Irresponsibility

Clothes

Curfew

Friends

Hair

Sex

Dating

Money

understand the stress in their lives, as you also remember that understanding is what you need to get what you want: peace and quiet at home.

 Mr. Obvious Wraps It Up in Case You Missed It: "Just do it! Whatever they are nagging you about, just go do it. The sooner you do it, the sooner they will stop nagging. No brainer! You want them to shut up, then get up and get it done."

Stupid Parent Note

Don't insult your parents for their "stupid" request. This only makes them madder. You might think what they want *is* stupid, but keep that to yourself and you'll save yourself a lot of stupid heartache.

Top 10 Ways Parents Embarrass You

Yelling at you in public

Dressing like a dork

Trying to be "cool"

Being too loud and drawing attention to them and you

Being too affectionate in public

Treating you like a little kid in front of your friends

Grilling your bf/gf

Saying something stupid in front of your friends

Drinking too much or doing drugs

Not taking care of their body

Mr. anD Mrs. EmBarrassing

Why parents do some of the things they do, I'll never know. And why they wear some of the stuff they wear is beyond me (see the cover for the worst case scenario). But parents will be parents, and that means that eventually they will totally embarrass you. So the question is, what do you do when your most embarrassing moment comes at the hands of your parents?

1. Remember that no one cares. The first thing to remember is that no one except you really cares about how weird your parents are. **When your friends' parents do something stupid, do you think any less of them?** No. In fact, you probably sympathize with them. You can understand their pain, but you don't associate what their parent did with them. You are old enough to understand that they are different people and **a dorky parent doesn't mean a dorky kid.** Besides, everyone has their own lives to deal with. Believe me, they aren't spending all their energy thinking about you and what your parent did. So get over it. If anything, it just gives everyone a good laugh. Growing older means becoming your own person. As you age you start to move farther and farther from your parents until eventually you literally move away. It's part of growing up; you can't always be attached at their hip. The same goes for your feelings. You can't feel attached at the hip emotionally to your parents' actions. They are separate individuals, and whatever they do is just that—whatever *they* do. No one thinks of you in the same way. So laugh it off, if you can.

Mr. Obvious says: "I care, I really do!"

2. Talk to them. If what they did is too heavy to be laughed at, then you might just need to talk to them. If they yelled at you in front of everyone, for example, then maybe it's time to talk to them alone and explain to them how that makes you feel and that you understand their anger but you'd appreciate it if next time they could save it till you got home. Remember, anger only escalates things, so be calm when you talk about this. If you want a fight, then scream and yell, but chances are you don't want a fight any more than they do, so calm down and talk like an adult. Don't let yourself get ramped up; it only makes things worse. Start a fight and not only are you embarrassed of them but you're now grounded, or getting the silent treatment, or having to listen to more yelling.

What I want you to get is that **you can greatly influence the outcome of situations by how you act and react.** A lot of kids feel helpless when it comes to their parents. They think they have no control over the relationship, but that's just not true. How you react to them greatly affects the situation. It's hard to have a one-sided fight. So if you don't allow yourself to get loud and angry, they won't have as much reason to fight. It's like this in all of life. You are 50 percent of the relationship. **You want to stop the fighting, then duh, stop fighting.**

3. Talk about them. Your parents might not understand that what they are doing is embarrassing you. A good way to help them get it is to **talk to them about their childhood.** See if you can't dig up some times when they were embarrassed by their parents. If they can sympathize with your plight, then they might actually get it and lay off a little. This isn't a science, so I can't guarantee you that it will work. But the worst case scenario is that you learn a little bit more about your parents' life and you bond more in the process.

4. Make a list. This works in all kinds of situations. When you have no power to change the way people act, you can start to change the way you think about the people who are acting weird. **Changing how you think can change how you feel,** and that's your goal, after all—not to feel so embarrassed of your parents. So here's an idea: Let's change the way you think about them **by making a list of the good stuff about them.** It can really help your mind. There are lots of good things about them; you just need to dig them up in your mind and put them down on paper to look at every time you think you're going to lose it because of the stupid stuff they do.

5. Give them time. A lot of times parents are doing stuff that embarrasses you because they just want to be closer to you. When you were little you needed them and wanted them around all the time. Now that you are getting older, you need more time to yourself. That's part of growing up, but don't forget about them. **They still want your attention.** So make some time for them.

Stupid Parent Note

If you wish your parents knew some of this stuff, give them this book to read. Or better yet, watch for *Not-So-Stupid Parents*, coming soon. If they read this stuff for themselves, it might make your life a little easier.

Do some things alone together. Go out to lunch once a week. Or go shopping. Do something that both of you like, just the two of you, so you can fill that void that they are trying to fill with their embarrassing moments.

6. Show them What Not to Wear. If they are totally out of touch in the wardrobe department, then send a video to TLC's *What Not to Wear* and get them a $5,000 shopping spree. But the truth is that what they wear isn't really that important to *your* life. Remember, it has no reflection on you in your friends' eyes. But if you want to help them out and help them get up-to-date, then show them some cool stuff. Remember, they aren't kids and shouldn't be dressing like you, but there are things that can hip them up a little. Take your dad shopping. I'm sure he'd love the input and the time alone with you. Talk to your mom about fashion and trends. It can be fun to give them a "what not to wear" of their own with just you. I know my mom and I loved our times together out finding her cute clothes. Sometimes parents are just too busy to take the time to find out what's cool, and other times they just don't have the skills to figure it out. So don't tell them how embarrassed you are of their clothes; just encourage them to find better stuff.

7. Get help. Your parents might be doing something totally bad, like getting drunk or high or taking their anger out on you in destructive ways. This kind of parent isn't as easy to negotiate with as some of the others, and you might feel helpless. If your parents are abusive, please talk to your teachers, the police, your pastor—whoever you know who can help them to get the help they need in order to be better parents. If they are using drugs or overdrinking, this is just as serious as physical abuse. You have to talk to someone, and you can't be afraid of what will happen. They need help, and you might be the only one who can get that for them.

Remember, as you get older, your parents are getting older too. And the thing about getting older is that once you start seeing your kid doing the fun stuff you used to do, you start to feel your age and hate it. You remember everything you could do when you were younger, and you miss it. The last thing you want to be is a boring *old person*. So **a lot of parents make up for the uncomfortable feeling by trying to act young.** Total embarrassment, I know. Why won't they just act their age? Face it, you don't like being thought of as boring or uncool, and sometimes your parents feel just the same. So they overcompensate so you and your friends won't dislike them. They have no clue it's so irritating to you.

It's not like your parents hate you and want to embarrass you wherever you go; it's just their personalities. And even though it's rough, you have to remember that you can't change anyone other than yourself. So **refuse to be embarrassed.** They are really no reflection on you. And half the time your friends don't see them in the same way you do. They might actually like their stupid jokes or their "hip" conversation. Just try to focus on the amazing fact that you have parents who love and protect you.

The Overprotective Parent

When you were a baby, having someone to take care of you and protect you was great. Your parents stopped you from burning your fingers on the stove and from drinking the Drano, but as you've gotten older, you've become pretty good at avoiding those things yourself. So **why do they continue to treat you like a baby?** "No, you can't go to the mall on your own." "You can't drive, date, or wear makeup till you're 18." "You have to be home every night by 10:00 p.m." "Button up your coat, and don't forget your hat!" And the list goes on. Overprotective parents can really make your life miserable. You feel like a little birdie who isn't allowed to leave the nest. Your wings ache, you see the other birds soaring by, and you want out so bad, but no go. "You're my baby. I can't let you do that. It's too dangerous." **All of their fears seem to run your life.** The fact of the matter is that they just aren't prepared for you to become a grown-up, which—news alert—there is no stopping. But from where they sit, they can't imagine that their baby has grown up so fast, and seeing you make the transition to independence can be hard for them. But unless they want you to stay at home forever and never move out, go to college, or start a family of your own, they are going to have to learn how to loosen up. And you're going to have to help them. So how do you start?

Act Your Age

Your job, as a teenager, is to start to become more and more your own person. That means you don't need your parents as much, you start making decisions on your own, and you handle the consequences that go along with those decisions. Some parents miss this crucial fact: You have to grow up. It isn't because they are stupid or because they want to punish you that they do the things they do; it's because they are worried. Worried they didn't teach you enough yet, worried that you can't take care of yourself, worried about the evil in this world and the dangers for their baby. So the best thing you can do is to start to alleviate their fears. How?

1. Agree with them. The best thing to do with an overprotective parent is to let them know that you understand their concerns. If you argue with them and tell them that it's stupid for them to worry about you going to the mall alone, they are going to continue to think that you are just too young to understand things. The key is to let them know that you get it. You are concerned about protecting yourself too; they aren't alone. Let them know you realize how dangerous it can be when you're at the mall with just your friends. Tell them that you know all about protecting yourself—not walking out to the car alone, not getting in a car with strangers, etc. **Whatever it is that they talk about being fearful of, let them know that you totally agree, that stuff is dangerous, and that's why you take so much care to avoid it.** When you agree with them rather than argue with them, they will slowly start to see your "maturity." And as that happens, they can start to feel more free to loosen the grip because they know that you have it all under control.

2. Accept responsibility. If you want them to treat you like an adult, then you have to start to move more toward your independence. That means you have to start to take responsibility for yourself and your actions. Things like cleaning up after yourself show a degree of maturity and independence. I mean, little kids need their parents to pick up after them and cook their meals. An adult can do those things on their own without whining about it. If you make a mistake, own up to it. That's a true sign of your ability to be mature and independent. If you run to your parents to fix things

My So-Called Online Life

With things like personal webpages, blogs, and social networking sites like myspace.com, parents have a whole new category of paranoia. All they hear about are the horror stories of kids being unsafe or stupid online. So here's what you do: Teach 'em. Show them your blog. Maybe even help them start their own. Tell them they can read yours whenever. Of course, if they can google, they can look at it even if you *don't* invite them. Since they have the power to pull the plug on your Internet access whenever they want, why not educate them so they don't get all freaky when they find out about your Web life? Besides, your openness and honesty builds trust. And with trust comes freedom!

you do wrong or trouble you get into, then you aren't exactly encouraging them to loosen up and let you do the things you want to do. The more you can do to show how responsible you are, the more likely they are to let you do the things you want to do.

Show Them You Can Be Trusted

Parents are overprotective because they worry that you can't take care of yourself. Your first order of business is to prove to them that you *can* be trusted. This is going to take some time, but it's the only way that you can get them to trust you and stop being so overprotective. Here are some basic ways.

1. Don't hide things from them. If they feel like you are hiding stuff, then they are more likely to try to control your life in order to protect you. So don't be all secretive. Keep your door open. Invite them into your room to talk. Share stuff with them, like your favorite music or hobby or whatever is unique to you. **Make them a part of your life,** and they'll be less likely to worry about you because they'll feel they know you inside and out.

2. Introduce them to your friends. The more they get to know your friends, the more they can trust you with them. If you have friends they don't know, they might start to imagine all kinds of horrible things you guys are doing together. **An informed parent is a more relaxed parent.**

3. Apologize. If you mess up and do something stupid or against the rules, apologize quickly. **Agree with them that you were wrong** and explain why you did what you did. Help them to understand that as you grow up, you will do more and more things independently, but they can trust you because you know the dangers out there and you know how to be careful.

Better Safe than Sorry

Share this list with your parents. Let them know you understand that life can be dangerous, but you know how to take precautions. That way they will learn to trust you more and more.

1. Make it hard on them. If a robber asks for your wallet and/or purse, *don't reach out and hand it to him*! Toss it away from you. More than likely he's more interested in *it* than you, and he will go for it. *When he does, run like mad in the other direction while screaming.*

2. Get seen. If you are ever thrown into the trunk of a car, kick out the back taillights, stick your arm out the hole, and start waving like crazy. The driver won't see you, but everybody else will. You can also look for the glow in the dark trunk release tab and pull it. Or move toward the front of the car and push on the back of the backseats to see if they release into the car.

3. Lock the doors. Girls especially tend to get into our cars after shopping, eating, working, etc., and start putting on lip gloss or digging for our phones. *Don't do this!* The bad guy will be watching you, and this is the perfect opportunity for him to get in on the passenger side, put a gun to your head, and tell you where to go. *As soon as you get into the car, lock the doors and leave.*

4. Don't go with them. If someone is in your car with a gun to your head, *do not drive off with them*! Instead, gun the engine and speed into anything you can, wrecking the car. Your air bag will save you. If the person is in the backseat, they will get the worst of it. As soon as the car crashes, bail out and run. It is better than having them find your body in a remote location. Another idea is to drive to the police station rather than where he asks you. Remind him that if he shoots you, the car will wreck and he'll get hurt.

5. Tips for when getting into your car in a parking lot or parking garage:

> Be aware. Look around you and look into your car at the passenger side floor and in the backseat.

> Avoid the van. If you are parked next to a big van, enter your car from the passenger door. An abductor can easily pull you into their van while you're getting into your car.

> Don't go it alone. Look at the car parked on the driver's side of your vehicle. If a male is sitting alone in the seat nearest your car (on the passenger side), you may want to walk back into the mall or your workplace and get a guard or policeman to walk you back out.

> *It's always better to be safe than sorry.* (And better paranoid than dead.)

6. No stairs. *Always* take the elevator instead of the stairs. Stairwells are horrible places to be alone and the perfect crime spot. This is especially true at night.

7. Stay out. If there is just one guy in the elevator, say, "I'll wait for the next one." You don't want to be alone in a small space with a potential bad guy.

8. Run. If the bad guy has a gun and you can run, *always run*! The bad guy will have a much harder time of hitting a moving target, and even if he does hit you, it most likely *will not* be a vital organ. Run in a zigzag pattern—that makes you the hardest to hit.

9. Let somebody else help them. Girls, don't be sympathetic to strangers. It can get you raped or killed. Ted Bundy, the serial killer, was a good-looking, well-educated guy who *always* played on the sympathies of unsuspecting women. He walked with a cane or a limp and often asked for help getting into his car or with his car, which was when he abducted his victims.

Why All the Yelling?

Some parents are yellers. Loud talkers. Out of control. And that's really it—they feel out of control. They don't know how to get you to do what they want, so they think that if they yell, they can get through to you better. It's like the foreigner who doesn't speak the language trying to ask for directions. He thinks that if he talks louder, somehow the person will understand him. It's just human nature. The more we think someone isn't listening or doesn't understand us, the louder we tend to get. That doesn't make it right or even make it better; it's just the way it seems to be. So what do you do with a yelling parent? How do you get them to quiet down? Depending on what's going on, it might help to remember several different things:

1. **Don't yell back.** When you yell back, you just give them permission to yell more. It's like you're saying, "Game on! Let's get this fight a-started!" And the yelling rages on. They should know this as well; if you are a yeller, then they need to figure out that yelling back at you isn't making you any quieter. It just starts a competition to see who can make the most noise and get the most attention. You have to shut up. Talk quietly. Bring the noise down.

2. **Talk calmly.** Both the talking and the calm are important here. You have to be careful about not shutting up completely. Don't sit there like a bump on a log saying nothing just to tick them off, because that's what you'll do—you'll tick them off, and then they'll just yell louder. You have to be smart if you want to change things at home. You can't keep doing what you're doing and expect a different result. That's nutso. So don't yell back and don't give them the silent treatment. Instead, answer their questions calmly. Take a deep breath if you need to in order to keep yourself from getting loud, and then answer them. In order to

control the situation, you have to control your mouth. Don't be smart or they'll yell more. Don't be mean or they'll yell more. And don't blame them or make excuses or they'll yell more.

3. **Give them a hug.** If your parents are grouchy and just taking things out on you, then change the pace and give them a hug. A lot of times they are just tired and frustrated. Affection can go a long way. So if they are just sounding worn out, sick and tired of being sick and tired, don't argue, don't fight back. Just walk up, give them a hug, and tell them you love them and you'll do whatever it is they want you to do. Then walk off and go do it. The yelling should stop immediately. In fact, the more hugs they get, the less likely they are to yell at all. But be real; don't patronize them by patting them on the back as if they are babies or laughing while you hug them. You have to be sincere, or they'll see right through you and just yell some more. They might be a bit shocked if this is unusual behavior for you, so give them some time to get used to it. Eventually they will start to trust you, and they should go easier on you because hugs help to take away stress. And less stress means a calmer parent.

4. **Stop.** A lot of times the reason parents yell is because you are driving them nuts. You know how it feels when someone does something you can't stand, like tap their fingers on their desk over and over while you're trying to think. Well, your parents can go crazy from stuff too. If you are doing something that repeatedly ticks them off and gets them yelling, then I hate to be Ms. Obvious, but *stop it!* What you do has a lot to do with how your parents act. So don't be a clown. Go into another room, stop doing whatever it is you are doing, or do whatever you can to just stop ticking them off.

5. **Listen.** Take time to listen to what they are saying. Sit down. Look them in the eyes. Even if you don't care, act like you do. I promise, it will make things go so much quicker, and then you can

get out of there. Now, I'm not trying to teach you to be hypocritical or insincere. Sometimes we do things we don't want to do. I mean, you don't want to get up and go to school some days, but you do anyway. And that's not being hypocritical. Even if you don't feel like listening to your parents, acting as if you do is much kinder than acting like you really feel. Loving someone doesn't always feel good and doesn't mean you just do whatever you feel. It means you put up with them sometimes. And the payoff from being kind and caring is always better than the results of acting like a jerk. So listen, even if you don't feel like it, and things will go much better with you.

Discounting Your Feelings

Sometimes parents just don't get it. They don't truly understand your feelings. Or worse yet, they think you shouldn't be feeling what you are feeling. It's hard when they tell you things like, "Oh, it's just puppy love; you'll get over it" or "It's not *that* bad." You know what you're feeling, and what you're feeling is major. It isn't anything that you'll get over soon or that you should stop feeling, so what is their problem?

It's true, your feelings are valid. You really feel them and they really hurt or feel really amazing. But the thing is that your parent has felt them too, just like you. Hard as it is to believe, they've had a major crush. They've been yelled at by their parents, neglected by their friends, and hurt by the one they love. They really *do* know what you are feeling in the sense that they've been there too, so why do they act like you shouldn't be feeling what you're feeling? See, it's been a while since they've felt the thing you are feeling, and they obviously are way over it—so they want you to realize that *you'll* get over it too. Trouble is, when they tell you it will pass, **they forget how much pain they had to feel before the same kind of agony passed for them.** They just jump right to the feeling better part and remember that. That's why they are telling you that in the grand scheme of things, this will soon be a distant memory. They are really trying to help but just not having too much luck at it. I'll talk this over with them in *Not-So-Stupid Parents*, but in the meantime, here are a couple things you need to remember.

1. Thank them. Thank them for reminding you that "this too shall pass." Tell them you understand that you *will* get over it, even if you don't feel like it right now. Then explain to them that even though you know you'll be better, right now you just really need to feel bad. That will help you to get over it quicker. We each have our own way of dealing with things, and right now this is yours. So promise them that you will look on the bright side, remember that time heals everything, and believe that everything will be all right—after you've had a good cry or some time alone with your game console.

2. Get them talking. This one might or might not work for you depending on your parents, but **getting them talking about themselves can be a great way to get them off the subject of you** and also to get them to remember how it felt to be a teenager. So ask them about the first time whatever it is that is happening to you happened to them. Ask them what they did, what their parents told them, and so on. This might not be of any concern to you at all, but it does have a way of getting them to change the subject. A lot of times all parents really need is to feel heard. **They want to be validated**—that is, told that they are right and that you get it and thank God for them, that kind of thing. They need to feel needed. So even if you don't feel like needing them, give it a shot. It could take the heat off and might even help you out with your situation. Best of all, it can remind them of their youth. And maybe through that they'll start to take your feelings more seriously.

3. Write them a letter. If you have a hard time talking over your feelings with your parentals, then change things up and write them a letter. **When someone takes the time to write something down nowadays, people have a tendency to pay more attention.** You can sometimes express yourself better alone in your room with a pen and paper than you can face-to-face. So tell them your feelings and how it hurts that they don't accept that you have your own feelings, even if they do seem irrational to them. But remember, validating some of the things they've said to you in the past is a smart move. They might seem crazy to you right now or you just might believe them, but either way, you can calm your parents' frazzled fear that you're going off the deep end of emotion. Writing it all down can help clear your mind and maybe even calm your nerves.

4. Learn to laugh. One of the most important things in all of life is to not take yourself too seriously. If you don't want any hassles with your parents, then learn to take it easy on yourself. What's happening to you might feel like the end of the world, or you might be feeling things you've never felt before—whatever it is that they are discounting, you have to practice laughing it off. This can help you in all areas of life, because from now on there will always be someone, somewhere, who won't validate your feelings. They'll think you've gone off the deep end or you're too emotional. Believe me, I know that of which I speak. Most of my life people have thought I'm a little out there emotionally. I'm passionate, and it can freak people out. But I had to learn to just get over worrying about what *they* think. I don't need others to validate how I feel . . . okay, maybe I do, but I've learned to find a few close friends who will sympathize with me and tell me I'm not crazy. As for the rest, I just expect them not to get me. So **don't get all freaked out when your parents aren't getting you.** Even though this might sound impossible, it is a goal worthy of your time and energy.

What to Do When They Just Don't Get You

If you don't feel like your parents understand, if they tell you that you don't or worse yet *can't* feel what you are feeling, don't fight it. Shut up. Tell them you understand their feelings, and then talk to someone who does understand. Some good alone time with God can be just the remedy for the misunderstood. Good music, pen and paper, and the good ol' Book will change your life in more ways than you can imagine. Think of this stupid time in your life as a call to drop everything and get close to God. When you truly have no one else who will listen and understand, God becomes the most real. So take advantage of the pain and use it to get next to God. Praying for your parents or even for yourself in dealing with them can really change your life. Believe me, it works.

6 Things Not to Do When They Think You're Crazy for Feeling What You Feel

- If you want to avoid an all-out fight over your feelings or just want them to stop with the lectures, then stay away from some surefire ways to just make things worse. That means:

- Don't scream "You just don't understand!"

- Don't try to *prove* to them that it's okay you feel the way you feel.

- Don't tell them they are just too old to understand.

- Don't try to hurt yourself to prove to them that you really are feeling what you say you're feeling.

- Don't give them the silent treatment.

- Don't argue with them over your right to feel.

The Big Talk

I know sometimes talking to your parents can be agony. They don't always get you. They think they do, but they don't. They have this image of you as a baby, sitting in your high chair and eating from a rubber spoon, and they just can't see the grown-up you, so they freak when you start to talk to them about important issues. They can be overprotective, scared of what you might say, deaf to what you want to say, or just plain stupid. Whatever the problem with parental communication, you can do a few things to help the process along. It's all about interacting with the people in authority in your life. The same stuff that works in a job or with a teacher works with parents. **You just have to know how to package your thoughts, yourself, and your words.** And in the end you might succeed in getting your point across more smoothly than usual and avoiding all kinds of arguments.

Getting Them to Trust You

Parents who trust you act a whole lot different than parents who don't trust you. Trust me! If they think you can't be trusted, they aren't going to be very good at listening to you. It's like they have a wall up and can't hear what you are really saying. What they are doing is interpreting what you are saying through the screen of doubt. If they don't trust you because you've lied to them before, then they have a tendency to be leery of your words. It's a human thing. It's like if you have a car that breaks down a lot, every time you drive it you are always thinking "What's that noise? Is it about ready to stall on me?" **You don't trust a broken-down car to run smoothly, and parents don't trust someone who has lied to them in the past.** So before you can expect your parents to have easygoing, smooth conversations with you, you first have to make sure you have the trust issue taken care of. Trouble is, trust isn't something that happens overnight. It takes lots of experiences over time to prove to them you are a radically different person. So you have to start now to show them that what you say is really what you mean, 'cuz that's what builds trust: doing what you say you're going to do.

I know it seems like a lot of work, but the payoff is major. Building trust is the best way to get what you want out of a relationship with anyone. No trust, no getting much of anything. And the good part is that it's all on your shoulders. You can build trust as much as you want to build it. Really successful people build it like crazy. They know that the more people who trust them, the more allies they have. And the more allies you have, the fewer and weaker your enemies. Trust goes a lot further in this world than doubt. So how do you build it? Here are a few ideas to think about.

Be Honest With Yourself

Seems like a no-brainer, but it's really not. If you can't be honest with yourself about yourself, then you can't be honest with anyone. And frankly, **people who lie to themselves look like idiots.** When you let yourself lie to yourself, you systematically destroy all your relationships, not just the one with your parents. Self-deception is a nasty thing. So get real and keep it real. This means that you take a long, hard look at who you are, how you treat others, and what you think about most often.

Who are you when no one is looking? If you think you're a trustworthy, honest, and reliable person, does that hold up when you really look at yourself? Are you really all of those things? Or are you two different people when you are alone and when you are with someone else?

Are you really all that trustworthy? You might get totally ticked when people don't trust you. But think about it—**would you trust you?** What's your true track record? Do you do what you say you'll do when you say you'll do it?

Why do you lie? Sometimes you might lie to yourself out of self-protection. You think that if you don't trust your parents, then you can't be hurt by them. But the truth is, **when you think the worst of people, you are more likely to get the worst from people.** You tend to get what you expect when it comes to others. Besides, think about how you feel when your parents don't trust you. They feel just as bad when you think *they* can't be trusted with your feelings. Their track record might not be the best, but you can help change that when you start to get honest with yourself.

Still not sure if you're being honest with yourself? Take this little quiz and see if it sheds any light.

1. I've lied to my parents:

   a. never

   b. once

   c. a few times

   d. more than a few times

2. When I say I'm going to do something, I do it:

   a. right away

   b. within a few days

   c. whenever I can get to it

3. I think my parents hate me.   True   False

4. I'm old enough to make my own decisions; I don't need my parents' advice.   True   False

5. I'm always right.   True   False

6. I don't need my parents. I can do life just fine on my own.   True   False

7. I owe my parents a lot for all they've done for me.   True   False

8. My parents never listen.   True   False

SCORING

1. a = 3, b = 2, c = 1, d = 4
2. a = 1, b = 2, c = 3
3. True = 2, False = 1
4. True = 2, False = 1
5. True = 3, False = 1
6. True = 3, False = 1
7. True = 1, False = 2
8. True = 3, False = 1

13–22: Less than honest. Bad news—you might not really be keeping it real. You have some really strong ideas that might be totally wrong. Try to look at life more honestly and dare to trust. Because if you can trust others to be honest, then you can start to be more honest with yourself.

8–12: Honesty is your policy. Sounds like you're pretty straight up with yourself, but be careful of those little lies you might tell yourself just to make yourself feel better. In the end, they only make you feel worse.

In the rare case that you are all about "keeping it real," beware, because **being honest doesn't mean being brutal.** Sometimes in the name of honesty people will say things that are downright mean. If what you are saying won't benefit the other person, then don't say it. If it's going to make them mad or hurt, you should probably avoid it. **If your sole goal is to be heard, to prove a point, or to be right, then you are dead wrong.** Keeping it real shouldn't be about being heard or winning; it should be about caring and honesty. So don't say things in the name of honesty when all you really want is to prove a point or take a shot at someone.

Keep It Real

Don't use honesty as an excuse to hurt someone. If you think you need to be "honest" with someone, first ask yourself these questions:

1. Is it the truth?
2. Will it help them to know it?
3. Is it kind to tell them?
4. Do I *have* to tell them because they are my parents or someone else in authority over me?

If you can't answer yes to these, then you might just be speaking out in order to make yourself feel better. Keeping it real is usually an excuse to say whatever we want even if it hurts someone else. Don't be selfish when it comes to honesty. If what you are saying will make you feel good but won't serve any purpose other than hurting someone, don't do it. Of course, when it comes to your parents, you are required to tell them what they need to know in order to take care of you.

Here are a few reasons *not* to tell someone something (aka Keeping It Kind):

1. If it will only hurt them
2. If they have no need to know
3. If you are only doing it to feel better about yourself
4. If it is a cruel thing to say

This one could be a no-brainer too, I guess, but I have to say it: Being honest doesn't just end with yourself. You have to be honest in all areas of your life. You can't just decide to be honest with your parents and not with your friends. You have to be the same person all the time, because those not-so-honest moments will catch up with you. It comes down to a matter of character. Who you are consistently is your character. And people decide how to treat you and react to you based on your character. Think about it like this: If your parents hear you lying to your friends on the phone by telling one friend you're busy with homework but then going out with another friend, they might start to question your character. **They think, "If she's lying to her friends, then she must be lying to me."**

Consistency also means you don't keep parts of your life shrouded in lies and other parts open to honesty. If you're an honest person, you're honest in all areas of your life. That means you're honest at home, in school, and in relationships with friends.

Your Trust Bank Account

Before you can expect to make withdrawals from your parents' "bank of trust," **you'll have to make a few deposits.** The more you do things to prove you can be trusted, the bigger your trust account gets with your parents. And the more the account fills up, the more loans they'll make you—that is, the more they will be willing to trust you in the future based on just your word. All this to say that the more times you are honest, the more power you will have in your life when it comes to your parents. When they can trust you, they start to let you make more decisions on your own, and they start to listen to you better. Honesty goes a long way.

It's All About Attitude

I always say **it isn't what happens to you but what you** *think* **about what happens to you that matters.** Your attitude toward your parents has a big effect on how well they are going to listen to you when you want to talk with them. So the question you have to ask yourself now is, "Am I causing the tension between my parents and me by the way I react to them?" If you can change your attitude and start to expect good things from talking to your parents, then good things might soon be coming your way. Here are some things to think about when it comes to your attitude in life. Ask yourself these questions to find out if you are reacting in ways that cause tension in your life:

Do you have drama in your life almost every day?

Do some people just grate on your last nerve?

Do bad things happen to you a lot?

Do you always seem to say the wrong thing?

Do you get in trouble a lot?

Are you moody?

Do you snap at people?

Do you distrust people?

If you answered yes to a lot of these, then you might just have an attitude problem. And the only way to fix things between you and your parents is to do something about it. "What?" you might growl. Glad you asked. *You have to change your attitude.* Always thinking the worst makes the worst more likely to come true. People don't feel comfortable around a grouch or a moody person. You don't make it easy to have a normal, peaceful conversation if you're overly emotional or grumpy.

If you want to start having easier conversations with your parents, then take a look at your attitude and give it some minor adjustments. **Attitude is your key to a happier home.** It might take a while for your parents to realize the change in you is for real, so don't expect them to think you're suddenly even-keeled and approachable overnight. Give them time to build up trust in the trust bank before you start to make any major withdrawals.

The Value of Memories

Building memories is a big part of building up that trust bank and building that bond between you and your parents so that communication gets easier. **When you can make the effort to do some stuff with them that will make for good memories, you are putting lots of trust cash into your account.** I know it probably sounds hokey, but if you want a better life at home, then you have to work at making memories. Do fun stuff with them: Clean the car with your dad and have a water fight. Bake cookies with your mom. Go on vacation and spend some alone time with them. **Talk to them about the memories of their childhood.** And take pictures—they help everyone remember the good times. The more you can bond with your parents, the more they will trust you and get you, and the better your life will be. I know they might seem impossibly boring right now, but the more memories you make with them, the happier they'll be, and the happier they are, well, the happier you'll be. Just try to think about how great it is that you actually *have* parents, as crazy as they might be. Things could be a lot worse.

Now, all this isn't some kind of parental propaganda. It's all about making your life better. If you want to be able to talk to your parents, then the brutal truth is that you'll have to put in the work.

Give Them Some Attention

You might not know this, or it may be painfully obvious, but the truth is that your parents crave your attention. Sometimes what can totally set them off and make them mad is when you never seem to have time for them. Remember, they still think of you as their baby and remember the days when you wanted to be with them 24 hours a day. And sometimes it can be hard for them to let go. **They miss you.** So if you notice that they get mad when you want to do things with your friends, things away from the house, things that they can't be involved in, then maybe it's time to pay them some attention.

Make time to spend with them. Eat dinner with them. Find a show you both like and watch it together. Go to the mall. Whatever it might be, just be with them. It might seem like time that you don't have to spare, but if you don't spare it, then the fights might just keep on going strong. Remember, this is all about fixing your life at home. If you want some peace and a better relationship with your parents, then you've got to find ways to change the things you've been doing. If you don't like the way things are, then you've got to change, because you are the only one you have the power to change.

One way you can show them some attention is by being happy for them. If something good happens in their life, celebrate with them. Send an e-card to their work email address. Bake them a cake, buy them a card, talk with them about it. If you think they don't want to share their wins with you, you're wrong. Everyone loves it when other people are happy for them. And it will draw you closer and help make some of those good memories. All of this will add up and make it so much easier for you to talk with them about *your* life when you need to.

Getting to know your parents is the best way to impact your relationship. It's so much easier to communicate when you really know each other. So spend some time and make the effort. I promise it will pay off.

Talk to Them

Now there's nothing left to do but the talking. When you've taken some time to work on yourself and your relationship with your parents, you'll find that approaching them to talk will be much easier. With some trust built and a good attitude from you, they will start thinking differently of you. Talking about deep stuff doesn't happen overnight, so before you get to the important news, spend some prep time learning how to communicate.

1. **Talk, talk, talk.** If you want to make it easier to talk to your parents, then put in the time and talk with them about stuff every day. It doesn't have to be deep stuff; just talk. Tell them about your day and ask about theirs. The more time you spend shooting the breeze, the easier it will be to talk with them when you have something big to talk about.

2. **Fill them in.** A good way to keep the conversations going the way you want is to fill your parents in. The more information you give them, the fewer questions they will have to ask, and the less you'll feel like you're being grilled. This is the best way to control the way the conversation flows. So talk to them about the things you are doing, like where you are going, who is driving, what you'll do there, and when you'll be back. Keeping them in the loop makes them feel more secure and adds a lot to the trust factor as well. Then when it's time to ask them an important question, they'll be less likely to blow up and more likely to listen.

3. **Control yourself.** When you want to talk to them about something important, you have to remember to keep things under control. Don't blow up all over them if they disagree with you. Keep your cool; it's the only way to help things go your way. Once tempers flare, all bets are off, and you lose any control of the conversation you might have had.

Some things to avoid: sarcasm, yelling, rolling your eyes, looking away, crossing your arms, huffing and puffing, growling.

Some things to do: Look 'em in the eye. Be calm. Listen. Give them a minute to process what you are telling them. Find points where you agree with them.

Setting Up the Big Talk

If you have something big to talk to them about and you aren't sure how they are going to react, then it's time to work on your plan. You don't want to just walk up to them totally unprepared and start dumping on them. So let's get to the planning so you can have the best opportunity to get what you want out of the conversation.

Timing is everything. No matter who you are talking to or what you are talking about, timing is everything. People who know how to get what they want know how to read situations to determine if the time is right to say what they want to say. It's like this: If your mom just got home, her arms are full of groceries, and she is moaning about her horrible day at work, it's probably not the best time to ask her if you can spend the weekend at the lake with your best friend. Wait until the time is right. **Make sure they aren't in the middle of something or upset about something** and you'll up your chances of being heard and getting your points across. If you have something major to talk to them about, you might even want to make an appointment. Parents can be really busy, and this might be the only way to get their undivided attention, so leave them a note asking for a time or ask them when they will have a sec to talk. But make sure they know that it's about something important. They need to be prepared as much as you do. For the really big stuff this is crucial. They need to be ready and able to focus, so pick your time and don't spring anything on them when they aren't calm and slightly prepared.

Rehearsal. Sometimes when you have something really big to tell them, you have no idea how to say it. So spend some time prepping. Write out your thoughts and get them straight. Think about what objections or arguments they might have and what you want to say to counter those. Believe it or not, sometimes the best way to counter an objection is to agree with it. This happens in sales situations and politics all the time. Admit your plan has flaws and that you can't get rid of all of their fears, but remind them that you're worthy of being trusted (you are, aren't you?). Once you have your thoughts together, do a dry run. Lock yourself in the bathroom and talk to the mirror. Getting ready for a big talk isn't a silly waste of time; sometimes it's the best way to ensure a good outcome. So give it some thought before you dump something big on them.

The note. If you are a better writer than talker when it comes to your emotions, write out what you want to say and give it to them to read. Stay there while they read it, and then afterward talk it over. Sometimes that's a better way to make sure they get all you want to say before they start to give you their two cents worth.

Take turns. After they've heard what you have to say, give them a chance to talk. Whatever you do, don't interrupt them or get mad at them. Bite your tongue and don't show your freaked-out-ness in your face, or you'll mess up any chance of having a calm conversation with them now or in the future. This is crucial for you to get: You are partially in control of how this relationship plays out. If you want to be free to talk to them about things, then control yourself when it's their turn to talk so that they will want to talk with you now and in the future. Think!

End it well. When you've heard their side of things and the conversation is over, end it well, even if you didn't get your way. One option is to say, "I can see that you're not convinced, but I don't want this to come between us. Would you promise me you'll just think about it some more?" and then say, "Thanks for listening." Even if they don't change their mind, if you can leave them feeling good about this talk with you, they'll be more likely to handle the next talk even better.

Having "The Talk"

If you want to talk to your parents about sex, it can be a scary thing—for you and for them. How do you even start? If you aren't sure where to begin or what to say, here are a few convo starters for you:

"I feel kind of weird because we're going to be talking about sex in school next week and I don't know anything about it."

"My friends were talking about sex today and they said (you fill in the blank). Is that true?"

"Sex is such a big issue that I thought I'd fill you in on what they are teaching us about it in class."

Getting Them to Say Yes

So what if you want to ask your parents for something but you're pretty sure the answer is going to be no? How do you get them to say yes when the chances are slim? The answer is that sometimes asking your parents for something involves a lot more than talking. The setup can be crucial. You have to think of yourself like a member of the special forces going into a foreign country for a special op. Prepare for possible scenarios. Set the stage so you are at your best when it's time to talk. **The time before the talk is just as important as the talk.** And what you do leading up to the talk will greatly impact the outcome. Let me give you a concrete example of how to talk to your parents about getting something you want but they might not be too keen on giving.

If you just can't live with the curfew you have but your parents won't budge, you've got to start today to prepare the way for getting what you want. **Asking for something this major is impossible without first filling up the trust bank.** The more you do these things *now*, the more they will be inclined to extend your curfew. So here's how it looks:

1. **Stay in touch.** If you can stay in touch and keep them informed as to what you are doing, they will learn to trust you more. I know it seems like they are overprotective and will never leave you alone, but the ironic truth is that the more you try to help them protect you, the more they will loosen up. So here's a few ways to stay in touch:

- Before you leave, **let them know where you are going,** who you'll be with, and what you'll be doing.
- When you are out, **give them a call before you come home. Let them know, "I'm just checking in. Wanted you to know** I'll be leaving for home in half an hour. See you later." This lets them know that you are responsible and understand how careful you need to be when you're out at night. Remember, you have to agree with them about their fears and concerns. Life *is* more dangerous for people who aren't aware of the things that could go wrong.
- Leave your cell phone on so they can contact you.

2. **Don't break the curfew you have.** If you want to be able to stay out later, don't miss your curfew. Sounds backward, but if you don't keep the one you have, then they won't trust you handle a later one. If you have a good track record of being trustworthy, then they are more likely to extend your curfew over time.

3. **Talk it out.** When you've done all these things for a good amount of time, you can start to talk to them about an extension. The amount of time you have to wait to do this varies depending on how trustworthy you've been up to now and how full your trust account is. Remember, if you want something, you have to work toward it. You have to prove yourself worthy in order to get what you want. Your parents don't owe you a better curfew. You have to earn it. It's just like life: You earn your grades, you earn your money, and you earn their trust. The sooner you realize that your actions greatly affect how you are treated, the sooner you can start to gain more control over your life. Parents aren't stupid, contrary to what this book title says. They know when you are ready for responsibility and when you aren't. So start to prove yourself today, and before you know it, you'll be getting more and more independence.

Overcoming Their Objections

When your parents won't let you have or do something that you think you are ready for, you have to prepare your case. Just like a salesman, you have to look at their objections, analyze them, and figure out how to overcome those objections. This means finding answers to their concerns so that they can be more open to the possibilities. It goes something like this. Let's say your parents won't let you get a cell phone. First of all, figure out their fears and make a list. What could concern them the most?

_____

_____

_____

_____

Okay, so you have your list. Now you have to figure out how to overcome these objections. Do this by deciding what you can do to make them understand that the things they fear won't come to pass. In the case of a cell phone, that goes something like this:

The bill. "I know you are worried about the cell bill, and I completely understand, so why don't we just get me some prepaid minutes. That way I won't be able to go over." Voila! Now they don't have to worry about big bills. Before you talk to them, decide what amount you think is best for you so you can talk it over.

Doing something dangerous or illicit. Let them know that you understand that cell phones can be dangerous if you text strangers, give your number out to people you meet online, and that kind of thing. Tell them that you know how worried that makes them, but let them know that they can track your calls on the bill each month. And if they think you're too young and are totally freaked, they can get you the Firefly phone that can only call 3 preprogrammed numbers. Heck, they can even manage your incoming calls.

Ways to Ask without Starting a Fight

How you approach "the ask" is way important. If you sound defensive, aggressive, defeatist, or anything negative going in, you can really taint their reaction. So try some of these pointers:

- Confirm with them that you understand their fears

- Agree with them about the dangers of whatever it might be

- Assure them you are ready to be responsible

- Offer them an option that could alleviate some of their fears

- Take baby steps to get you closer to what you want

- Prove to them you can be trusted in the little things

When you think that your parents' thoughts are stupid,

they get defensive and are even less likely to give you what you want. So the key is to sympathize with their concerns. See things from their point of view and tell them that you get it and that you want to help get rid of their concerns by doing this, that, or the other. You have to become a problem solver so your parents can start to see that you can handle things and be trusted. So put some time and effort into it, and you might just see a change in their attitude.

Talking too much. This one's hard to argue because it's more than likely true. The best way to fight this argument is to agree to prepaid minutes. You could also tell them, "Yeah, I know I talk on the phone too much, but this way you can have the home phone to yourself. I'll never be hogging it anymore because I'll have my own phone, and you won't have to take any messages for me anymore either."

Playing with it in class. Tell them that you understand that concern and that your teacher has a strict policy on that and you don't want to get it confiscated, so you promise to leave it in your locker or leave it turned off during class.

It will spoil you. This is one you have to prove to them by not being a spoiled brat. If other stuff spoils you, then they have good reason to believe this will too. One argument is to let them know that it's a safety thing. If your car ever breaks down or you need to reach them, you can call because you'll have a cell phone. It's not a luxury, it's a safety thing!

It would be nice if talking to your parents was as easy as talking to your best friend, but that's not always the case. And that doesn't make them bad parents or you a bad kid; it's just normal. It can be hard for parents to remember what it was like to be your age. They have to deal with their own stressful lives and don't always think about *your* feelings. But whatever the dilemma, you have to tell yourself that they don't mean to be so stupid, they just don't know how to be any different. And if you want things to change, then it's up to you. Remember, in any relationship where someone is in authority over you, **you have to be smart about communicating with them in order to get things to turn out the way you want them to.** Relationships aren't smooth and easy all the time. You can learn a ton about yourself and life by maneuvering through the rough parts. So quit your complaining and get to work! You *can* have a better relationship with your parents.

Know Your Authority Figure

Negotiating can drive parents crazy, so you have to be careful about this one. You can't be too obvious. The key is to find out their conditions casually. You do this best by just getting to know them. Find out what the ground rules are for things like parties, concerts, trips, etc., before any of them ever come up. This way neither of you will get too heated about the topic when it does. The better you know your parents, the better you can figure out what you can and can't do.

For example, if you know that going to a concert is off-limits, talk to them about why. Find out what their fears are and what, if anything, would ever change their mind. Don't make this a time to argue your reasons; just to do some recon. You have to be smart. It's much better to prepare for a mission than to walk into an ambush. So get some intel. If your friend is in a band and will be playing downtown next week but you know your parents don't like you to go to concerts because they are too dangerous, think about ways to overcome their objections. What if they were to go to the concert too? I know, it could be a disaster, but what if they didn't stand next to you? Would it be worth it? Or what if they just came along and hung out in the restaurant next door? Or would they let you go as long as your big sister was with you? Think it over. Give them some options, but go in with the mind-set that if they say no, then so be it; you gave it your best shot. Because remember, when people are in authority over you, all the screaming in the world won't give you more power. You have to deal with the situation at hand using the tools at hand.

ReBuilding Broken Trust

PART 4

You've gone and done it: You've

blown it with your parents, and now they say they'll never trust you again. Ouch! That's not a good thing to hear. And although I'm sure you think it's true that they'll *never* trust you again, that doesn't have to be the case. But face it, broken trust takes a long time to rebuild. It's like you've withdrawn every last bit of trust from the trust bank account, and you are now overdrawn. Things aren't looking too good. So what do you do now? I mean, how do you ever get your freedom or their respect back? There are a few things you can do—no, let me rephrase that—*must* do or things aren't going to change.

Mr. Obvious says:
"Even if you don't think
what you did was stupid now, trust
me, one day you just might!"

Fessing Up

The first thing you have to do is admit you've done something wrong. You can't ignore that fact. You have to come clean. That's the first step in getting things back to the way they were. If you don't admit it and call your mistake a mistake, then your parents will think you haven't learned anything. Agreeing with them that what you did was wrong and being truly sorry goes a long way toward helping them to think there is hope for you and you *can* learn and grow and change and be trusted once again. Accepting responsibility is the first step in recovering your parents' trust.

Giving Them Time

The second thing on your plate is living with the consequences. What you did probably had results. The car you wrecked has to be paid for. The class you skipped has to be retaken, and the people you hurt, namely, your parents, have to be healed. See, when you broke their trust, you did something to their heart. You caused them to erect a barrier around it. They do this to protect themselves from being hurt again or abused again by your actions. Because that's how they feel: abused, as if what you did was done directly to them. It's a normal parental feeling. And that's why they lose their trust in you—because they've been burned. Because of that you have to give them time to heal, to get over it. And I mean *time*, because that is what it will take. **They can't just forget about it overnight.** So don't be in a hurry to fix things. Over time things will seem less and less huge to them, and your relationship will get better. Just remember that you can't rush it and you can't rush them by whining to them about getting over it and moving on. Give them the time they need.

ReBuilDing the Trust

The next thing you have to do is rebuild. Trust doesn't come without a lot of work, like I've already said. So hunker down and get ready to do some heavy lifting. Just tell yourself, "This is what I have to do in order to get my freedom back." You can't resent their new rules and restrictions, because you caused them yourself. So do all you can to accept them with a smile. Don't buck and say you won't do what they are now asking, because **the quicker you do what they ask, the quicker trust can start to be rebuilt.**

Getting Over It

Losing your parents' trust can be devastating, but it happens. Don't make matters worse by getting mad at yourself. Sure, say what you did was wrong, but then move toward a change. Don't mope around the house in utter despair; that's not going to fix anything. **Living in the past and hating yourself for what you did is destructive and doesn't accomplish anything.** A lot of times you are moping as a way of punishing yourself. Nutso! Don't do it. Talk about destructive! Your parents have the punishment part under control. That's their job, and I'm sure they're doing it well, so let go and move on. Hanging onto your past mistakes isn't a pattern you want to get stuck in, or it will become bondage for the rest of your life.

The best way to get free of a giant mistake is to give it to God. He's big enough to take it, and that's what he does. He takes away our junk. So fess up to him what you did, and thank him for his forgiveness. Then get over yourself and get on to a changed life. Focus on what you want and how to get there, and start moving.

It's also important to know that mistakes aren't all bad. They are allowed to happen so that we can learn from them. So don't miss out on the good that can come from them by wallowing only in the bad.

Changing Things

The final step in rebuilding trust is to make sure that what you did never happens again. Because if it does, then any trust you have rebuilt will go out the window, and gaining it back will be twice as hard as before. Your job is to do what you've got to do to make a difference in your life. If you keep missing class because you can't get up in the morning, then find a way to change that. Go to bed earlier. Move your alarm across the room. Ask your mom to come in and open the curtains. Whatever it takes, **don't keep making the same mistakes over and over again and expect your parents to trust you.** They'd really be stupid if they did.

Really Stupid Parents

We've talked a lot about

the ways your parents treat you—things they do to you, say to you, and make you do that can make you nuts. But what about those things they do to themselves, things that can't be helped by changing your thoughts or actions? How do you handle it when good parents go bad? It's not your fault when they mess up. It sometimes has nothing at all to do with you, but that doesn't make it any easier. **You get caught up in their drama by mere association.** And sometimes there's no escape from the really stupid parent.

The Hurt of Divorce

When I was 11, my parents got divorced. I didn't think much of it at first. Since I was an only child, I guess I was too busy trying to take care of each of them to think about what it meant to me. The drama in their lives was agonizing. They needed someone to be calm and in control, and that was me. I remember at that point consciously deciding that I now had to be the leader of the family. I had to take care of things because my dad was no longer going to be there. So I bucked up and became "the man of the house," at least in my mind. And my childhood ended.

Their divorce had nothing to do with me. I mean, it was all about their inability to get along. But that didn't mean I wasn't changed forever by it. Divorce sucks, plain and simple. It's never easy to deal with. It never leaves you untouched. At first I dealt with the trauma by hating my dad. He was the one who messed up; it was his fault, I reasoned, so I hated him. I was so protective of my mom that I couldn't see that it takes two to tango. I had no idea until I got a lot, lot older that **this wasn't my battle to fight or take sides in.** My job was to live my life and live it with both parents, even if that meant doing a lot of traveling. But instead I cut myself off from my dad and spent years without him. That did a lot of damage to my mind and my heart. Not until much later was I able to finally forgive him, let go of my anger, and reconnect with him. Now we get along great. I just wish I hadn't missed all those years of having a dad. So what could I have done differently? How could I have had a better relationship with both parents who did a really stupid thing? Here are some things you can do that might help. I didn't figure it out till way too late, but it's not too late for you to save your relationship with your parents.

It's Not aBout You

The first thing to convince yourself of is that **this divorce is in no way about you.** It's about a man and a woman breaking up. It's their relationship that has gone south. It's their problem, their stupidity, that's made them make the worst mistake of your life. Sure, it might seem like the best thing they could do for themselves. But for you it's disaster. I know. But it is something they are doing for themselves. So believe me when I tell you that it isn't about *you*.

The biggest thing that helped me get over my parents' divorce and get back to loving them both was realizing that **they are only human.** I used to think my dad was like Superman or something. He was my idol. I followed him around wherever he went. In my eyes he could do no wrong. So when he left, I felt like he was leaving me, although I didn't realize it right away. I knew it wasn't my fault, but I thought that if he loved me, no matter what happened with him and my mom, he would never leave *me*. But he left, so I must not have been special enough to make him stay, right? Wrong. That lie tormented my life for many years. If only I had been old enough to understand that it wasn't about me, things could have been so much better. I could have had a life with my dad. But instead I chose to hate, and I hurt both him and me.

Before I got married, I had broken up with a lot of guys. I'd tried to make it work many times and seen my efforts fail. Face it, making someone stay with you isn't easy. You have differences, things one or both of you just can't live with, and so the breakup happens. Parents are no different. They feel like the relationship they are in just can't go on. They can't possibly live with one another any longer, so no matter who else is affected, they split up. They reason with themselves that it's better for you to live in a peaceful house with one parent than an angry house with two.

They really *do* think that what they are doing is for the best, even though you are sure that it isn't. They really have no concept of what it is doing to you. And a big reason for that is that it isn't about you. They aren't divorcing because of you. They are divorcing *each other*, not you. So don't let yourself believe any longer the lie that it has anything to do with you. If you can see them as only human and see their *relationship* as the real issue, then you can start to be free from a good deal of their divorce trauma.

Don't Break Up With Either of Them

Once you can convince yourself that it isn't about you, you have to make a conscious effort not to break up with either of them. They are both still your parents, and both should be part of your life. That means **you might have to make a major effort to stay connected to the one you don't live with.** And sometimes that effort might seem one-sided, but don't give up. They need to know that you don't blame them and you still want a relationship with them. So call them when you can. Send an email, a card, a note, whatever. Just do what you can to stay in touch.

Forgive Them

This is a big one. But the thing to remember is this: When you won't forgive someone, you allow the pain they inflicted on you to remain a gaping wound exposed to the elements. **Unforgiveness hurts only you.** You might think it's the best way to get back at them, but it really does nothing to them at all. When you forgive, you can heal. Forgiveness seals up your wound and makes you whole again. It's like this: Anyone you can't forgive, you can't stop thinking about. And when you can't stop thinking about them, you keep reliving the injury over and over in your mind. It might as well be happening to you again and again. Then you're never free from them. If you want to be free from the pain, you have to forgive them and get over it. Move on. That's the only way you can heal.

You have to forgive your parents for being stupid. They were just plain stupid when they got divorced. They weren't attacking you or doing something to you on purpose, so you don't have to forgive them for being mean but for being human. If you can remember that they are only human and not the superheroes you thought they were when you were little, you can be free to forgive them.

How do you forgive? First it's important to **understand the definition of forgiveness.** According to Webster's dictionary, to forgive means "to give up resentment of or claim to requital for" or **"to cease to feel resentment against."** Forgiveness **doesn't mean you tell them that it was a good idea that they split up.** It doesn't even mean you say, "It's okay you got divorced," because the truth is that it *isn't* okay they got divorced. Divorce is never okay. What forgiveness does mean is that you are going to stop resenting them for it. You are going to get over it. Because if you don't get over it, then you'll be haunted by it until you do.

Some parents might make this harder than others. They might move away from you, avoid you, or straight out tell you that they don't want to see you. But even in these horrible situations, you have to remember that it still isn't about you, it's about them. They are messed up, not you. They aren't avoiding you as much as they are avoiding responsibility. These kinds of parents are a real special kind of stupid. They need your prayers more than your hatred, because hatred only destroys *you*, not them.

Mr. Obvious says:
"Stupidity IS a forgivable offense."

I know that one parent probably looks the guiltiest, like they messed up more than the other, but looks can be deceiving. In a relationship it always takes two. They each played a part in the biggest mistake of their lives. And **if you try to pick sides, you only supersize their mistake.** So in order to keep the drama to a minimum, you really have to try not to pick sides. When one of them starts to slam the other one in front of you, you have to do your best to stay neutral. Tell them you'd rather not get in the middle of it. They probably won't listen, but you have to try. Then you have to avoid the blame game. Don't tell the other one what the mad one said. Don't take the battles on yourself. In fact, do all you can to stay out of earshot of the slamfests. **The less you hear, the happier you'll be.**

Not picking sides **also means not becoming the mediator between the two.** You don't have to be the messenger in their continuing battle. If they want to say something to each other, let them say it themselves or write it in a note you can deliver. But tell them you'd rather not pick sides or get involved in their war because you need the love of both your parents in order to have a healthy life.

Life Isn't Over

You might feel like a monster truck has run up on your life and pinned it to the wall, but that doesn't have to be the case. Your life can go on—in fact, it must. Keeping focused on your goals, your hopes, and your dreams can help keep your mind clear. Spend some time writing out your dreams. Think about what you want to do, where you want to go, and who you want to be. This divorce will be not the death of you but the birth of you, if you let it. Use the negative for good. Trials and tribulations, if accepted as something good, can only make you stronger. The most successful people in the world aren't people who have had blessed lives but people who have lived through turmoil and destruction and come out on the other side. So focus on your future, not the past, and let this stupid mess become a step toward the next big thing in your life.

Talk It Out

The biggest and best way to work out anything in your life is on your knees. Spend time talking out your pain and anger with God. Whether you pray by your bed or spend time journaling, the more you do this, the more you'll be free from the stupid choices made for you by your parents.

You can also talk to someone like a counselor or pastor. Sometimes just telling another person how you feel can make you feel a whole heck of a lot better. Just make sure that you aren't using this as an excuse to wallow in your pain. Getting over things sometimes means giving it up to God, trusting him that he'll work this junk out for you, and then getting on with your life.

Divorce is never a happy thing. And it should never happen in your life, but it does happen. Trust me when I say you can live through it and make it to the other side. You can have a good relationship with both parents, in most cases, and you can learn to trust again. Don't let their stupid mistake become your future. Choose to forgive them and get over it so you don't end up repeating it yourself when you grow up.

The Harm of Drugs and Alcohol

In most households the parents are trying to keep their kids from using, but in some it's the other way around. If your parents are under the influence of drugs or alcohol, your life can be miserable. I'm sure you feel helpless, and in most instances you are. You are at the mercy of their ever-changing moods. It's something no kid should have to live with. So what do you do if your parents are using drugs or alcohol?

Talk to someone. You weren't supposed to have parents who get high. It's not normal to live in a household where the adults are doing drugs or getting drunk. They are there to take care of you, not vice versa. You need to talk to someone about your parents. Contact a counselor, pastor, police officer, or whoever you can find to help you through this. Talk in order to make sense of your life, but also talk in order to stop the insanity. If your parents are using illegal drugs, then they are endangering you and need serious help. See if you can find an adult who can help you through this and be there for you when you need them.

Don't try to fix them. Although you can talk to someone about this, you have to know that you can't fix your parents. You don't have the power, no matter how hard you try, to change them. They have to want to change themselves. You might have tried to control them and failed. That's to be expected. Drug and alcohol abuse is a tough battle to fight, and it shouldn't have to be yours. The thing to remember is that you can only control yourself. Choose not to follow in their footsteps. Decide to get out and get things done. Stay active. Join groups at school. Stay clean. When you try to manage your parents' life, you are fighting a losing battle. So don't feel guilty if you can't help them; it's not your fault and it's not your job.

Find a support group. There are groups out there that can help. Talk to your school counselor, pastor, or social worker. They can help you find a support group near you. It helps to talk to other kids who are going or have gone through the same trauma.

If your parents are addicted to drugs or alcohol, you are 4 times more likely to become addicted if you choose to drink alcohol or use illegal drugs.

(Source: National Association for Children of Alcoholics, www.nacoa.org)

1 in 4 kids under 18 lives in a family where a person abuses alcohol or suffers from alcoholism.

(Source: National Association for Children of Alcoholics, www.nacoa.org)

Alateen is a group for teenagers who are affected by someone else's alcohol or drug use. It holds meetings, like a club, where young people share tips on how to make their lives easier when a family member drinks too much or uses drugs. The meetings are sponsored by Al-Anon. You can find the location of meetings near you by looking in the phone book under Al-Anon or Alateen, or you can ask your school counselor, a clergy member, your doctor, or another adult you trust to help you find meetings near you. Another way to find out about Alateen is by logging onto their website at www.alateen.org or calling toll-free at 1-888-425-2666.

(Source: National Association for Children of Alcoholics, www.nacoa.org)

The Hypocrisy of Materialism

Drug abuse and divorce seem like pretty obvious and stupid parental blunders. But there's another kind of stupid parent that is more subtle. These parents aren't abusive or mean. They aren't drunk or fighting. They just aren't there. In fact, you rarely see them. You let yourself in the house. You make your own meals. Do your own thing. It might seem kind of cool to your friends, but deep down you really wish you had a better relationship with one or both of your parents. But **it seems like working is more important to them than you are.** This is **the materialist**—the parent who is **so obsessed with having things and giving you things that they seem to forget they are parents.** Their entire focus is on work and making money. And it's not all bad; after all, they *do* buy you tons of things. Anything you want, really. In fact, they say, "I work so hard so I can give you the things you need." It's out of love for you that they are working so hard, they reason. But the truth is that you need your parents more than you need *things.* It's the hypocrisy of materialism at work.

So what do you do about the materialistic parent? Well, just like other kinds of parents, the materialist can't be changed if they don't want to change. You can't control what they do or how they do it, but you can let them know how you feel and pray that it will make some kind of impact on them. **Most materialistic parents think they are doing you a favor.** Somewhere along the way they got confused about what kids need. When you were little they saw all the clothes and toys you "needed," and they felt inadequate. They decided then and there that you wouldn't lack the things they lacked, so they put the nose to the grindstone and went to work. Maybe they needed a second income to afford day care or braces, or maybe they just wanted a nicer car. Whatever it was, somewhere along the way things got out of control and that human desire for more took over. Now they are so obsessed with things they haven't even considered what that obsession is doing to you. So talk to them. **Help them to understand what you need from a parent and what you don't need.** This isn't a time to cut them down but to love on them. Tell them how much you like being with them and how much you miss them. **Let them know that you have enough things and that you would much rather never get another new outfit than continue to miss them every day.** Whatever you feel, let them know about it. They might just be thinking that you love *things* as much as they do so you want them to keep working all the time. So have an open discussion with them. They may or may not see the light and make some major changes in their life, but either way, at least you've done what you can.

The next thing you can do is make an effort to get into their schedule. If they can't quite swallow the "please work less so I can spend time with you" plea, then you might have to try something more intrusive. Get on their calendar, but make sure it isn't for an event centered around spending money. This is where the truth comes out. Do you really want *them* more than *things*? If you do, then come up with some free stuff you can do together. The more you take money from them, the more you show them that they have to continue to work hard to support you. So it's time to think about your life and what is important to you. Things or people. Love or money. Try writing out your thoughts. Tell your parents how you really feel about them and about the things they provide. Do your best to live a life without being materialistic, and see if you can't help them to come to the light side.

Living With a Single Parent

If your parents split, living with just your mom or just your dad can be totally different than living with both parents. You might notice the change instantly or you might not even think about it, but things can get all upside down once one parent moves out. I know for me it was really weird not having my dad around anymore, but I wasn't totally crushed or anything. It was just my life. He wasn't there that much when they were married anyway, so no big difference. Of course, after a few years things started to pop up in my life where I really felt like I needed my dad, and when he wasn't there, **I got pretty resentful.** But fortunately we worked through that stuff—or should I say, *I* worked through that stuff. He's not much of a talker, but that's okay; I get him now and we see each other regularly.

But back to my story. **Living with just my mom was a good experience. We are best friends now,** and I think it has a lot to do with us doing life on our own. But as I look back I can see a few things that maybe weren't the best situation for a kid growing up. I don't resent her for it; she didn't know any better. She was just doing the best she could. We both have grown over time and have come to understand more about the importance of the family and the roles of the family. But way back then we just didn't know the best way to do things, so we did what came naturally. We became best friends.

A lot of parents feel like their kid is their only ally in the battle with their ex. Not only that, but they are so upset from losing their mate that they get really freaked out about losing you too. So to make sure that you don't skip out on them too, either physically or emotionally, they tend to make decisions that won't get you too upset. They might make decisions because they want you to be happy so you'll like them more. That's an old trick of the divorced parent. They want to make you think life with them is great so that you won't leave and also so that you'll tell your other parent how great they are. That way, they secretly hope, the other parent will feel regret for what they did and see what they are missing out on. I mean, it's just what all of us tend to want to do when we break up. We want the ex to regret the terrible decision they made. We want them to come crawling back to us, begging for forgiveness, because they see how happy we are or how much fun we were to be with. Even if we have long since moved on from the breakup, when we've been rejected, something inside of us still always wants the rejecter to feel remorse over not having us anymore. So we do all we can to try to make them feel as awful as possible about leaving us. It's human nature. But that doesn't make it right or even healthy. The goal shouldn't be to hurt the other person as badly as they hurt us but to take care of ourselves and heal up from the emotional trauma of a bad breakup.

That said, it doesn't always happen that way. So mom wants you to tell dad how happy she is and how much fun you two are having in your new lives. She doesn't want him to think she is depressed or that things at home might not be good, so she does what she thinks will help her image, and that is to make sure that

you are as happy as can be and have nothing to complain about. What she does is become your best friend.

I know for me that's totally how it went. **My mom and I were best buds.** I didn't have to do anything around the house that a normal kid did. I didn't have chores. I didn't have to cook, or do dishes, or even clean up my room if I didn't want. I know, sounds dreamy, huh? But wait, there's more. We talked about everything together. She knew all of the stuff going on in my life, and I knew all the stuff in her life. And it was great. I really do have good memories of growing up. But there are a few negative things that can come (and for me did come) out of that kind of parent/child relationship.

The biggest negative I can remember was **feeling the void of a parental figure.** I mean, if you'd asked me if I felt safe, I guess I'd have had to say, "Not really." And I know exactly why. After the divorce my mom started dating this guy. He was an okay guy, I guess. Kind of creepy thinking of your mom dating, but hey, what can you do? But the bummer part was when they broke up. I guess he hurt her pretty bad, because she was a wreck. I can remember her crying for days. She was so sad. I felt so awful for her. I was her shoulder to cry on, like any best friend would be, and so I heard all the pain of a jilted lover. I can remember at that point making a decision. I was about 13 years old, and I said to myself, "Well, it's time for me to step up and take charge. The one who should be parenting isn't in any state to do it, so I'll have to do it." I remember being so concerned for my mother that I started thinking of all the things I should do to take care of her. Essentially, I looked at all the things my dad did around the house and decided I would start doing them. I remember thinking something totally stupid. I said to myself, "Well, I can start changing the lightbulbs and fixing the toilet when it breaks." Why I thought of those two things first, I have no idea. But it seemed like a good place to start—to start to become the parent, that is.

The Best Friend Parent

And **therein lies the problem with becoming best friends with your single parent.** When things get bad for them, they come running to you, and you shouldn't have to bear that kind of responsibility. Being the child of divorce can really age you fast. It makes you grow up much more quickly than other kids because you have to—there's a void to be filled, and you are the only one there to fill it. Or at least that's what it feels like. Of course, I am an only child, so I took on all the burden myself, but in families with more than one kid, the oldest often takes on a parental role. That's totally wrong because then you are not only parenting your parent but also the other kids. I know sometimes that's the only option, though, and if it is and you've stepped up, I totally applaud you for it. But my hope is that your parents will read this book or get ahold of **Not-So-Stupid Parents** (the adult version of this book) and read for themselves that what you need is a parent, not a best friend.

Don't get me wrong: I love having my mom as my best friend now, and I think a close relationship with your parents is awesome. I just hope that you will get to be a kid too. So I guess the deal is, don't jump so fast to take over. **Don't tell yourself that the burden of parenting is now yours,** because it isn't. Your mom or dad might seem totally messed up right now, but they will get over it. They'll heal, and they'll be strong once again. If they need help, maybe you can suggest that they talk to someone at church or a counselor or something, or even go to a support group. Great divorce care groups are popping up in churches all over the country, and they're a great way for adults to share each other's problems instead of laying them on you. My philosophy is that you are entitled to respect and love your parents, both of them, even if one hurt the other really bad—that's *their* deal, not yours. So you shouldn't have to hate the other one for them. That's just not helping anything.

So what do you do if you can tell that the parent you are living with is trying to be your best bud? The first thing you have to do is decide that you don't want your relationship to be that way. And that's quite a decision, because what a great home environment. They don't argue and fight with you as much as other parents; they aren't all bossy; they are cool and laid-back. A great life . . . or so it seems on the surface. But you have to remember that along with that peace comes the other stuff I've just talked about. And if you can see the forest for the trees, then you'll need to believe that **you need a *parent* and not a best friend.**

Once you've decided that, then you'll have to convince Mom or Dad. The best way to do that is to tell them that you don't want to be involved in the fight between them and your other parent anymore. Let them know that you don't want to be their courier, taking emotional bombs into the enemy camp, helping to destroy your other parent. Let them know that you need to respect the other parent and that when they share all their feelings about them with you, it's hard for you to do so. **You don't want to divorce your other parent; you want to have a complete life, not a broken one.** It might be hard for them to catch on to this idea, so you might have to remind them, "I'm not getting in the middle of your fight." But over time most parents will get it and stop coming to you with their grief.

Your first response might be to feel like you are betraying their need for you, but you have to stop that thinking right now. You are the kid, not the counselor, and you are entitled to **be** the kid until you become a grown-up. So no feeling guilty for asking to be treated like the kid that you are.

Another thing to do if you sense the best friend parenting approach would be to help their worried minds by letting them

Family Feud

For me, not only my mom but also her entire family hated my dad. I can remember listening to my grandmother and aunt tell me how awful he was and how he didn't do this and he didn't do that. It was a slamfest every time they were around, as if I would take all that info back to him and shove it in his face so that he would hurt even more. What they didn't get is that the only person they hurt was me. They gave me a skewed image of my dad that wasn't true. He was only human, he made mistakes, but I didn't deserve to be emotionally dadless because of their hatred for him. See, I took what they said and internalized it, and I decided I hated him too. So for 5 years I didn't talk to him. I even changed my name. I didn't want anything to do with such an awful man. How I hate that I did that! I love my dad. He was once my hero, and in a lot of ways he is again. I just wish I hadn't lost those 5 years thinking I had to feel as awful about him as the rest of my family did.

know that you aren't planning on moving out at the first problem or disagreement. Help them to understand that your relationship with them isn't going to fall apart the first time they make a parental move, or even a stupid move for that matter. Give them freedom to be the parents they were meant to be so that you can be who you were meant to be.

Avoiding the best friend parent bomb can be tough for both you and your parent, but eventually you'll see what I mean if you haven't already. Parents were made to parent, not to become our best buds. So let them do their job, and I pray they will let you do yours, because being a kid is the best thing in the world, and I don't want you to miss out on it!

When your Parents start Dating

If one or both of your parents have started to date, you'll have to to **be prepared for their dating drama.** Most parents, especially the "best friend" parent, like to talk about the ins and outs of their dating life with their teenagers. They must feel like you are all in the same boat since you are in your dating years too. But it's not always the most fun thing to think about your mom or dad being romantic with someone. There are some things you just don't want to know.

You don't have to feel like the family counselor when it comes to your parents' extracurricular activities. In fact, I don't even believe their dating drama should be a part of your life. As a kid you start to feel one of two things when your parents start to date. You either feel like you're losing their love and attention to a stranger, or you feel like your parents are reverting back to their teen years and becoming hormonally charged kids again, losing control of all their senses. In that scenario it can be kind of hard to respect them and see them as the more mature one of the family. Either way, **getting involved in their dating life isn't the best thing for your relationship with them.** They might think it's essential to keep you involved—I mean, what if they marry this person? You have to like them too. But the trouble is, what if they break up with this person after you've grown to love them? Then you have to go through the loss of divorce all over again. So if your parents are dating, I hope they have a look at this chapter. And I hope you both make a few crucial decisions about your involvement in their love life. It's important to the health of your childhood and teen years to be kept out of the dating drama of the people in your life who should bring stability and safety. Leave the subject of puppy love and heartache to you

and your siblings, and let the grown-ups find other grown-ups to share their misery with.

So if your parent wants you to get involved in their dating life, let them know that it isn't something you want on your shoulders and that you'd like to be kept out of it as much as possible. Let them know that you support them and their pursuit of love, but you'd prefer to just have to deal with your **own** love life and not your parent's.

Maybe your parent will get the picture, or they might just keep going on with life as usual. Either way, let me just tell you, you will survive. Things **will** get better. And things will definitely change. It might be really hard right now, but in time things should mellow out, and hey, you might end up with a really cool stepparent. No matter what the outcome, just remember that no one can **make** you feel anything. What you feel is up to you. The power is in your hands. So if you are sick of feeling the way you do, then change what you think about. Concentrate on something new, like your future, and let your parents live the drama they have created for themselves. They aren't your responsibility anymore!

When I was about 14, my dad married my *first* stepmother. She was only about 10 years older than me, had no kids, and didn't want any, especially me. For the next 13 years she made my life miserable. I hate to say it, but I cried on the day he married her and I smiled on the day she left him. Now I have another stepmom who is a million times better. She is actually the one who helped restore my relationship with my dad. So you see, **steps can be really great for the family!** She works really hard to keep us communicating, and she does all she can to make me part of their new family. So when it comes to stepparents, I've lived through both kinds, the bad and the good. When I was younger I didn't really know what to do with a mean stepmom. There weren't any books like this around, and it was such a new thing for me that I had no idea how to deal with the potential jealousy and resentment. And so I ran. I ran from my first stepmom *and* from my dad. But now I'm older and wiser, and I have a few ideas about how I would do it if I had it to do all over again.

60% of second marriages end in divorce

Robert E. Emery, *Marriage, Divorce, and Children's Adjustment* (Thousand Oaks, CA: Sage Publications, 1999).

Just because your dad picked her out, got down on his knee, asked her to marry him, and moved her in doesn't mean you had any say in the matter. Chances are you had **no** say. He fell in love and that was that, and now you've got a new mom. Well, not really, but she sure looks like a mom. I mean, she lives with your dad. She sleeps in his bed. Eats dinner with him. Watches TV each night with him. Goes to family functions with him. She does all the stuff your mom used to do, but that doesn't make her your mom. So what about when she tells you what to do? What about when you don't like her rules or her way of doing things? Can you revolt? Call for a mutiny, or better yet a new stepmom? Boy, I wished I could have way back when my dad married wife #2. But you can't do any of those things. Suddenly there's a new sheriff in town, and you had no part in the election. So what do you do when they tell you what to do? Do you say, "You're not my mom!" and run out of the room? Do you complain to your dad about how evil she is? Or do you give up all that your mother taught you and start to live as your step-monster, I mean stepmother, has decided you will live?

3/4 of divorced men and 2/3 of divorced women remarry

Robert E. Emery, *Marriage, Divorce, and Children's Adjustment* (Thousand Oaks, CA: Sage Publications, 1999).

Well, my answer goes something like this: Remember that thing I said about living under authority? And how you can't overthrow your parents or quit them? Well, same goes for steps. They aren't (and might never feel like) your parent, but **while you live in what is now their house, you have to live under their secondary authority.** Of course, your biological parent is your real authority, but they have decided that this new person is the kind of person that they can trust not only with their heart but with you as well. So the deal is, if you want peace in the home, then you can't buck and kick every time your step asks you to do something. You have to decide that learning to live under authority is the best option for your mental health. You don't have to like the way they do things; all you have to do is remember that the best way to make this relationship work is to go with the flow. No two homes are the same, so I guarantee you that this step won't run things the way your other parent runs them. Things will seem awkward, not normal, and I totally understand. Heck, to me, my stepparents' households never felt like home, but I never had to live with them full-time. I always got to go back to normalsville with my mom. But if you have to live with your step full-time, then take heart, because things will eventually settle in. It will begin to be home to you. Not the home you were used to but a new home. Just remember, if you want a fight you can always get a fight, but do you really want your home to be a war zone?

Everything you've read in this book till now applies to the stepparent, because it's their home you are living in now. Even though they aren't the boss of you, they are the boss of the household. So practice what you've read and know that ultimately it isn't about how things get better or whether they ever get you or not, but it's about you and your character. What you learn and put into practice in this home will help shape your life. You can't be in charge of who your parents marry, but you can be in charge of how you react to them. And **your reaction has a huge effect on what they do and say to you.** The payoff from respecting your step, even if deep down you resent them, is huge. A resented step is not the best person to live with, but when you set them free from your anger, you can start toward a happier home life.

So here's the deal: You have to forgive them. I know that they might be the reason your parents broke up. They might be totally awful and horrible to live with. They might want all of your parent's attention. But whatever the trauma, you have to forgive them. If you don't, then you'll resent them, and resentment makes for a nasty home life. It's like something rotten under your bed just stinking up the place—it only gets worse and worse with time. So you've got to do some spring-cleaning. Decide to get over the offense they committed in exchange for happiness. I mean, you can hang onto your anger, but you're the only one you're hurting. Sure, you might make things uncomfortable for your step, but you're living in your own personal hell until you can get over whatever it was they did or are doing to you or the ones you love.

Who knows? Maybe if I had made a bigger effort to get to know and care for my first stepmom, she would have been nicer to me. She might have seen that I was not her enemy but her ally. She might have grown to be a good friend. But no use crying over spilled opportunity. I believe that we tend to get out of people what we expect to get out of them. If you think highly of people, they are more likely to treat you kindly than if you think poorly of them. Our thoughts really do have a lot to do with how people interact with us.

The Competition for Attention

A lot of times stepparents feel a little jealous of their spouse's kids. They feel like their spouse loves the kids more than

in 1992, 15% of all children were living with biological mother and stepfather and 1% were living with biological father and stepmother

Robert E. Emery, *Marriage, Divorce, and Children's Adjustment* (Thousand Oaks, CA: Sage Publications, 1999).

they do. And the spouse probably does. I mean, you are their flesh and blood, and that is irreplaceable. It's too bad stepparents can't always understand that your relationship and their relationship to your parent aren't the same. You will never replace the step, and the step will never replace you. But alas, they don't always get that. I know my first stepmom was very jealous. She saw my involvement with my dad as competition. She didn't want him to love me more than he loved her. It was kind of weird, I thought. But in the end I let her win and I left him to her. Big mistake.

I think **stepparents the world over struggle with jealousy.** It's got to be hard for them, seeing someone else get the kind of love from their spouse that they want to get. That's one of the dangers of marrying someone with kids: You never truly get the person all to yourself. You know how it is when you're dating someone—how you just want them all to yourself and how you can get jealous when they do stuff with their friends and such. Well, it's the same in the adult world, and so many a stepparent gets jealous over the relationship their spouse has with someone else.

Stepdads can also have problems because of their competitive nature. Perhaps they aren't as prone to jealousy as stepmoms, but they might compete for your mom's attention. Either way, steps can be a lot to deal with when it comes to the time and love of your parent.

But sometimes the jealousy is on the other foot, and you feel totally jealous of your stepparent and the time they spend with your parent. The thing you have to remember is that no matter how much your parent loves this new person in their life, that person can never replace you. You will always be their kid, their flesh and blood, even if for the time being it seems they are totally obsessed with their new love. And besides, there really is enough love to go around. It isn't always the step's fault either; sometimes your parent might be the one overcompensating by taking some of the time they used to have for you and giving it to their spouse.

The best way for you to deal with jealousy is to try to understand where everyone is coming from. If you can get that your

"'You shall love the Lord your God with all your heart, and with all your soul, and with all your mind.' This is the great and foremost commandment. The second is like it: 'You shall love your neighbor as yourself.' On these two commandments depend all the Law and the Prophets."

—Jesus in Matthew chapter 22, verses 37–40 NASB

step fears losing out on your mom or dad's love and that your parent is hoping to make a better life for himself or herself with this person, then you can start to get outside of yourself. When you can understand where another person is coming from, you can deal with them a whole lot better. If you can come to terms with the fact that things are different now and your parent's time is going to be split between you and this new person, then you can start to allow them that time to be together. And hopefully the step will start to allow you time with your parent as well. It might not seem like it right now, but there is always hope. Things don't often stay the same. And if you are willing to give love and consideration when you aren't getting any in return, you are one step closer to changing things. Someone has to be the bigger person here and make the move to improve things, and it just might have to be you.

Love is an amazing tool in the hands of someone who knows how to use it. When people feel loved and respected, they tend to soften up. So don't be so quick to hate, but look for opportunities to care for others. It's no surprise that the two greatest commandments both include love. It truly is what makes changes in the world we live in. So find ways today that you can love without getting anything in return. The payoff will one day come and the change will happen. But even if it doesn't, I guarantee you that loving on this side of heaven will only make heaven that much better for you! So stay focused on what's best; don't break under the pressure of hatred and resentment. Let love win the fight, and things will change before your eyes.

The End

"No one can drive us crazy
unless we give them the keys."

—Doug Horton

Well, our time together is over.

I hope you've found something you can take from all this. I know your parents can really be a hassle to live with and figure out, but that's the only option that really makes sense, if you think about it. They can be your biggest fan and your most loving support if you give them the chance. It might not seem like it right now, but it *can* be that way someday if you put in the effort.

Here's the thing: **It isn't what *happens* to you but what you *think* about what happens to you that matters.** You can either call it a loss and live the rest of your life in a continual battle with your family, or you can look at this as an opportunity to learn something that can improve the rest of your life. **The ball is in your court.** Although it might not seem like you have a lot of say in your life right now, the truth is that you are the only one who really *does* have control over you. That's because **you have complete control of what you think and therefore of how you feel.** No one can make you *feel* anything you don't choose to feel. Now's the time to start taking responsibility for your own life and feelings. You can choose to be happy, and you can choose to create peace around you if you are willing to put in the work.

Take this little tour through the mind of your parents as your opportunity to change your life. You can do it, I know you can. If you apply the principles in this book to your life, you will have a huge head start toward living more happily whenever you're under authority. And that means happier in school, happier on the job, and yes, happier at home.

Let me leave you with this one last thought: **The older you get, the easier it gets to deal with parents.** And the closer you'll get to them too. If you can keep from burning too many bridges now, you'll see that your relationship with them *after* you are out on your own can be totally amazing. **They're a lot like you,** ya know—that's why it can be hard living together. But it's also what can bond you together and in the end makes it so you totally get each other. You just have to make it through these years of you wanting to test your wings and them making sure you don't go *splat*. If you think about it, that's not so stupid.

A particular train of thought persisted in, be it good or bad, cannot fail to produce results. A man cannot directly choose his circumstances, but he can choose his thoughts, and so indirectly, yet surely, shape his circumstances.

—James Allen, *As a Man Thinketh*

Hayley DiMarco writes cutting-edge and bestselling books including *Mean Girls: Facing Your Beauty Turned Beast, Marriable: Taking the Desperate Out of Dating, Dateable: Are You? Are They?, The Dateable Rules,* and *The Dirt on Breaking Up.* Her goal is to give practical answers for life's problems and encourage girls to form stronger spiritual lives. From traveling the world with a French theater troupe to working for a little shoe company called Nike, Hayley has seen a lot of life and decided to make a difference in her world. Hayley is Chief Creative Officer and founder of Hungry Planet, an independent publishing imprint and communications company that feeds the world's appetite for truth. Hungry Planet helps organizations understand and reach the multitasking mind-set, while Hungry Planet books tackle life's everyday issues with a distinctly modern spiritual voice.

To keep the conversation going log on to
www.notsostupidparents.com.

And for more on Hayley's other books check out
www.hungryplanet.net.

"Feeding the World's Appetite for Truth"

What makes Hungry Planet books different?
Every Hungry Planet book attacks the senses of the reader with a postmodern mind-set (both visually and mentally) in a way unlike most books in the marketplace. Attention to every detail from physical appearance (book size, titling, cover, and interior design) to message (content and author's voice) helps Hungry Planet books connect with the more "visual" reader in ways that ordinary books can't.

With writing and packaging content for the young adult and "hip adult" markets, Hungry Planet books combine cutting-edge design with felt-need topics, all the while injecting a much-needed spiritual voice.

Why are publishers so eager to work with Hungry Planet?
Because of the innovative success and profitable track record of HP projects from the bestselling *Dateable* and *Mean Girls* to the Gold Medallion-nominated *The Dirt on Sex* (part of HP's The Dirt series). Publishers also take notice of HP founder Hayley DiMarco's past success in creating big ideas like the "Biblezine" concept while she was brand manager for Thomas Nelson Publishers' teen book division.

How does Hungry Planet come up with such big ideas?
Hayley and HP general manager/husband Michael DiMarco tend to create their best ideas at mealtime, which in the DiMarco household is around five times a day. Once the big idea and scope of the topic are established, the couple decides either to write the content themselves or find an up-and-coming author with a passion for the topic. HP then partners with a publisher to create the book.

How do I find out more about Hungry Planet?
Use the Web, silly—www.hungryplanet.net

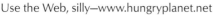

WARNING!
The average teenager should not attempt dating before reading these manuals!

the
dateable
a guide to the sexes
rules

Justin Lookadoo and Hayley Morgan DiMarco

Dateable:
are you?
are they?

Justin Lookadoo and Hayley DiMarco

Available at your local bookstore

CAUTION:

These books are almost too hot to handle.

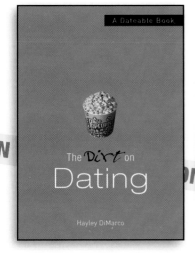

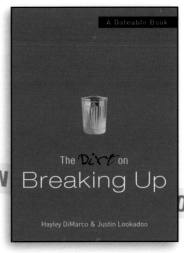

It's real. It's raw. It's true. **It's the Dirt.**

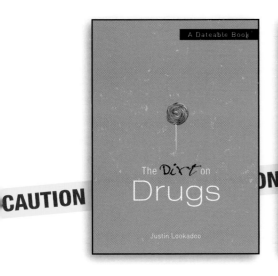

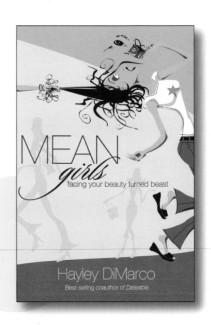
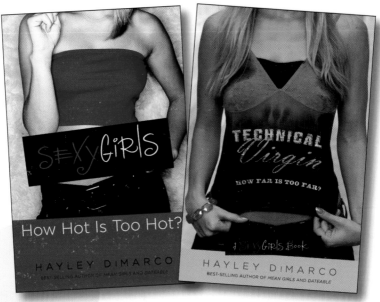

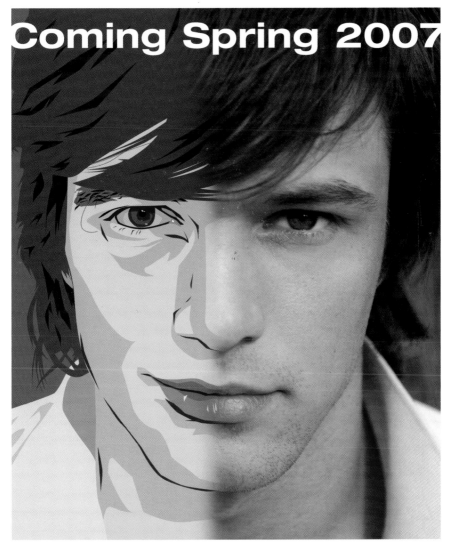

Coming Spring 2007

The Man Manual:
Mastering the Moves, Power-Ups, and
Pitfalls to Becoming a Real Man

Revell
www.revellbooks.com

www.hungryplanet.net

Hey youthleaders!

✔ Check out www.hungryplanet.net to find your free, downloadable discussion guides and retreat guides for these books:

Hey parents!

COMING SPRING 2007

Why Your Kid Thinks You're Weird and How to Prove Otherwise